AEGEAN SUN:

The Airport

Stephanie Wood

ISBN-13: 9798672644288

The Aegean Sun series of books:

Room 101

The After Effects

The Diaries

Room 102

The Office

The Wedding

Rooms and Revelations

The High Street

A Pair of Summer Shorts

The Airport

The Kafenion

Grace's Story

CONTENTS

APRIL

'Oh, here we go,' Stelios thought as the noisy crowd of holiday reps tumbled out of the people carrier which had brought them from the aeroplane to the arrivals hall and into his domain - Passport Control.

'I can't find my passport!'

'I think I've left my iPad on the plane!'

'Nooo, my Coca-Cola's leaked all over my bag!'

He'd heard it all before, and worse, so he tried to ignore the ones making a scene at the back while he checked through the more sensible and coordinated ones in front of him. It was the same every year: some reps were experienced travellers and had everything in order, others were either new or just plain stupid and couldn't even organise themselves, never mind a rowdy rabble of holidaymakers. He occasionally saw those same reps passing back through the airport the other way before the season had even officially started.

He vaguely recognised some of them as they had worked there the previous year, but he had never really chatted to them and definitely didn't know any names so he studied each and every passport carefully as he checked the details through and finally gave a nod of recognition to Mark, the Head Rep, who he knew was reliable and had just proved as much by sorting out the other reps' current issues quickly and without fuss.

'OK, look, everyone just wait here for the luggage and I'll go and check if Elias has arrived and find out what transport has been arranged to take us to the hotel,' Mark informed the rest of them as they drifted around the baggage reclaim area. 'Maybe have a little look around because, unless something major happens during the season, you probably won't get to see this area again and it's good to know what facilities are here in case of any complaints.'

'Oh, way to bring the mood down, Mark!' Russell called out. 'We've been here five minutes and you're already talking complaints. I'll have you know I got no complaints from Kardamena last year and I can guarantee it will be the same this year, thank you very mush...'

'Sit down Russell,' Mark said quietly as he approached the boy, 'and drink some more water before we go out to the coach. I don't want you throwing up again like you did on the plane.'

'OK boss,' he replied sarcastically as he sat down and reluctantly obeyed orders.

Mark went to the meeting area but couldn't see Elias, the agency owner, though he could make out several coaches in the car park. Unfortunately, none of them seemed to be waiting for him as all was in darkness and the coaches out front were for the Dutch passengers.

'What's occurring?' Jane asked with a lazy Welsh

accent and a smirk.

'Nothing,' Mark replied to his good friend and colleague who worked with Elias in the office.

'Is he not here yet? Do you think there's something wrong?' she asked with concern.

'Oh, he'll be out somewhere having fun and lost track of time most likely.'

'Hmm, yeah, that does sound like him,' she nodded, 'but what about the coach?'

'That's what I'm worried about. One or other of them not showing can be explained, but for neither of them to be here seems very odd.'

'You'll have to call him and give him a nudge.'

'Yeah, I will. Surely he's just in some bar or other but if he's totally forgotten he won't like me waking him up at… what is it?' he asked as he checked his watch. 'Half past one?'

'Actually, it's half past three with the extra two hours ahead…' Jane grimaced.

'Yikes! But, then, that's not really our fault is it? I gave him the details and he's supposed to be here with the coach so he can't blame me for anything.'

'You did let him know the change in arrangements? That we were coming in from Amsterdam rather than Athens?'

'Yes, definitely. I sent an email and a text to make sure he knew.'

'Well, something's happened, so you'd better find him before World War 3 erupts in there when the effects of the alcohol wear off!'

She returned to the baggage reclaim carousel which was starting to rotate with one of the reps enjoying the ride and waving to everyone as he passed by.

Jane worried how that behaviour would look to the

Dutch reps, whose season had already started, as they hovered at the meeting point to wait for the arrival of their guests. She hoped that the very little they could see through the perspex glass at the edge of the area wouldn't include a view of the inebriated British reps, who didn't have the greatest reputation at the best of times.

Luckily the luggage started to arrive at that point so her colleagues all hustled themselves forward to collect their bags and cases as she retrieved the checklist of extra boxes which the company had included on their flight for transportation to resort. It had been a tricky operation to unload them from the BA flight in Amsterdam to transfer them to their Kos flight, even with all the extra hands to assist, but at least this time it would be just a simple case of loading them straight onto the coach – as long as it turned up.

'Aargh, look at my case!' one of the new reps shouted as she dragged a very heavy looking blue sparkly case off the carousel.

Jane couldn't see a problem but went over to quell the panic.

'There's a humungous gash across the top. Oh, it's ruined,' she exclaimed, dragging out the last word into a long wail.

'Has it pierced through the surface?' Jane asked sympathetically as she approached.

'Yeah, something's sliced through it and ruined my lovely case,' the girl whimpered.

Jane turned the case to see the damage, but didn't see anything initially.

'Show me what's happened,' she instructed, trying to remain supportive while not seeing any problem at all.

'Here, see? Something has slashed it and spoiled the whole effect.'

'Hmm. This scratch here?' Jane asked as she just about spotted a small scratch which had in no way damaged the case and was actually almost impossible to spot. Unless you were the owner.

'Yes, right on the top. Oh, I love that case and now it's ruined.'

'Well, they do throw them around to load and unload so the odd scratch can happen quite easily,' Jane offered, but the scowl she received in return made her backtrack immediately. 'Of course, I will write a report and let them know what happened so they know you are upset about it.'

'I'm not upset, I'm devastated,' she spat back.

Jane realised that as a newbie, this rep would have no experience of the difficulties and pitfalls of travel and the likely combination of nerves and vodka would be a big contribution to her reaction in this matter. If she could reassure the girl just now, by the time she had slept on it and woken up sober to experience the gorgeous Greek sunshine tomorrow, no doubt it would all be forgotten. Also, she hoped it might help in the future if a guest found themselves in a similar position, she would be more understanding of how that disappointment felt.

'Yes, I know it must be horrible, especially right at the beginning of this amazing summer you're going to have, but at least everything inside is safe so once you get all your bits and pieces out in your room it will all seem much better. I'll take care of the report to make them aware of how it's affected you and I'm sure they'll feel just awful about it and hope you can still have a great summer here in Kos.'

'Mmm. OK. Er, thanks,' she replied as Jane's words instantly soothed her anger and despair like cold water being poured over hot ashes. There was still a bit of steam there, but it was quickly disappearing as reality set in.

A bemused Jane turned away to hide her smile just as Mark approached with an equally bewildered expression on his own face.

'So, what's the news?' she asked, biting her lip in anticipation.

'We'll get sorted one way or another, but it's gonna take a while. I gave Elias all our details, but he saw our departure time from Amsterdam of 7pm and knew we were arriving on Tuesday and presumed we were landing Tuesday night, not leaving Monday night and arriving Tuesday morning.'

'Didn't he check with the airport for the arrival?'

'Well no, not yet as he somehow got it in his head for Tuesday night. He said he was going to check our progress right through from London later this afternoon. What a dufus!'

'So what happens now?'

'Well he was in bed after all, so he's getting dressed and driving down here while he tries to sort out a coach to take us all up to the Kosta Palace. He knows Antonis and Sakis were out on the town last night so he's going to try Savvas and Petros first to see if he can get one of them to pick us up.'

'Oh, wow. OK, that's going to take a while then.'

'Yep. I told him to check the hotel reservations too because if he's messed that up, we'll have no rooms ready to stay in for our first week induction course.'

'Oh no! Will we have to go somewhere else?'

'Maybe, but that will be on Elias. There's plenty of

hotels and apartments he can use for tonight, but they just won't be set up ready for making a good impression on the reps. Anyway, hopefully he's forwarded my information on to them so they'll have the right details. He's going to get back to me. Soon, hopefully.'

'Soooo… What about…?' Jane half asked as she tipped her head backwards towards the area where the reps were still collecting their cases and joking around.

'Looks like most of the Dutch holidaymakers have already gone, so I'll wait until it's just us and I'll let the reps know there's a slight delay. We can pack up the boxes outside so they're ready to be loaded up once the coach arrives. By then I should know a bit more about timings and location.'

'Though the reps don't know which hotel we were going to, do they?'

'No, but they do know it's one of our top hotels where they're staying for a week of training before resort orientation.'

'D'ya know what?' Jane asked with droopy eyes and a resigned shrug. 'I don't think they'll give a monkey's if they can just get in bed and sleep for now. I think all this bravado is just about wearing itself out and they're ready to give up and settle down any time now.'

'Well, let's hope we all get loaded up onto the coach and delivered to some nice warm rooms before they all nod off,' he laughed. 'Or we'll be like the walking dead!'

Mark waited until the tourists had cleared the arrivals area and then asked the reps to assist with moving the boxes to the paved area outside so they would be ready when the coach arrived. By the time they had a system in place Elias had arrived and confirmed that Petros was on his way in the coach and that Kosta Palace did have the required rooms ready as they had been in possession of the original documentation showing the correct dates and timings.

'I'm so sorry Mark, I don't know how I got mixed up. Anyway, Petros is coming and everything is in order.'

'It's fine, Elias. At least everything is sorted now. You were probably reading so many different contracts and information that it would be easy to misunderstand.' *Or you just quickly glanced without taking proper notice of the details…*

'But I should be on top of things like that, so it won't happen again. Anyway, everyone seems happy enough for the moment,' he surmised as he nodded over to the reps who were jumping up and down trying to keep warm in the cold night air as the airport officials had closed the doors behind them.

'Well, the sooner we get to the hotel the better. I think they're all about to run out of steam and I'm definitely ready for bed. We've got a busy week ahead.'

'Yes, I am looking forward to meeting everyone properly at our special dinner at the end of the week. It's always a great way to get to know the reps before the real business starts. I've booked a great place near the square this time; we don't want all the skinny-dipping problems that we had last year, eh?' Elias laughed nervously as they were reminded of the moment when he'd got in his car to leave the party and turned on the headlights to reveal several naked reps and coach drivers happily frolicking in the sea in the mistaken belief that a moonless night would hide their assets.

'Hmm,' Mark agreed with a smile. 'Best to avoid temptation if at all possible.'

'Yes, much safer in the square.'

Mark doubted that, as there were many little

avenues and hiding places on all edges of the square where a rep could get up to mischief, but at least there was less chance of stripping off in public. Less chance was better than no chance...

'Ah, here is Petros,' Elias announced as the coach headlights appeared at the entrance of the car park. 'So, I will leave you now and see you in the office in the next few days?'

'Yes, I'll see you then.'

'Goodnight then. Goodnight Jane,' he called over to her and made a quick getaway in his car without waiting for her response, or for Petros' arrival.

There were whistles and whoops as the coach pulled up and after all the people and luggage and boxes were loaded carefully, the merry group made their way down to the resort, though most of them were asleep before they reached the main road.

After the first week of group induction, then another week of individual resort orientation, the reps were finally ready to receive the first guests of the summer season. As well as being the Head Rep for the island, Mark also covered Airport Controller duties, so he was determined to make sure everyone knew their responsibilities to avoid any difficulties down the line.

'We'll start in departures because, believe it or not, next week some of today's arrivals will be going home again,' he laughed.

'I suppose it will be an empty flight going back today then?' Naomi asked. Jane had finally managed to stop calling her 'sparkly case girl' and was glad that the 'incident' on arrival had easily been forgotten.

'Probably not. Some of the islanders and expats use this flight to visit family and friends at home before it starts to get busy. It's usually much cheaper than normal.'

'Doesn't look like there's much of a queue,' she pouted as they approached the empty check-in desk.

'Well it won't be full, or probably even half full, but it won't be completely empty. Anyway, next week we'll bring people through to queue up to this point here,' he indicated the end of the zig zag system, 'and keep the rest of the queue outside to allow this area in-between as a corridor for passengers to move around.'

'So, we just have to keep the rest of them entertained in the sunshine while they're waiting to come in,' Russell informed the rest of the group.

'Thank you, Russell. Yes, we need one person to stay at the head of the queue to make sure everyone knows what's happening and no independent travellers just wander in on their own and cut into the line, but other than that it's helpful if others walk up and down the line to reassure the people waiting and maybe check that they've handed in their customer questionnaire.'

'Or you can fill it in for them instead,' Russell whispered to the reps he'd worked with before who smiled knowingly.

'After they've checked in,' Mark continued, 'they put their cases through the scanner on the right which puts it on the conveyor belt system and out to the sorting area. Next to that is a spiral staircase down to the toilets, but try to get them to go straight through passport control at the end as there are more toilets in there.'

'So, if they want to have something to eat or go to the loo, we just kind of shove them through?' Naomi asked with alarm.

'Not at all. I mean let them know the procedure on

the coach before you bring them in, like we did in those practices, yeah?'

She nodded uncertainly.

'They'll know to check in, then drop their cases, then head through passport control and you can stress that all the facilities they will need are there, including toilets, café and duty-free.'

'But there's a kiosk right there selling food and stuff,' she pointed to the Everest counter under the departures board.

'Of course, and you can't actually stop them, but if you remind them that they can't take any bottles of liquid through with them, they're more likely just to buy what they need on the other side. That way we know everyone's gone through and we don't end up searching for people locked in the loos, or sitting outside somewhere with a sandwich. It's just much easier on everyone.'

'Ah, OK. I get it,' she nodded.

'Right. This is where they'll queue up for Passport Control, but if the line gets too long one of the airport security team will split the line here,' he pointed to a red line on the floor, 'and then form the rest of the queue outside again. You don't need to worry about this unless they ask for help directly which will probably be just until they can get reinforcements.'

'Hang on,' another rep interrupted. 'They have to go back outside to queue up again?'

'Possibly. It only really happens when there are a few flights checking in together, but this is the system they came up with last year and it worked, mostly.'

'Apart from some of the Geordies kicking off,' Russell laughed.

'Yes, well, it wasn't perfect, but hopefully it will work

better this year as the extension they're building now will be completed at some stage during the summer and things will be easier then.'

'Except they said that last year too,' Russell reminded him.

'But this year it's definitely going to happen, so just keep an eye on how things work and by peak season it should be plain sailing. Anyhow,' he began quickly before Russell could say anything else, 'someone will be going along the line to check the guests' boarding cards, then they will have to put their stuff in trays for x-ray and walk through the scanners. It's important to go through this procedure too on the coach because we've had a lot of feedback about the fact that they will pick up their belongings and straight away be faced with passport control, without any real area to repack any stuff they've removed. It's better if they can repack their bags while the trays are still lined up, or they will have to juggle all their bits and pieces in their hands as they give in their passport to security.'

'Hey, I could show them how I juggle my bits and pieces in my hands,' Russell laughed.

'Seen it all before,' his fellow rep joked. 'Not impressed.'

'Yes, very funny,' Mark nodded. He wasn't against a bit of fun among colleagues, but they were all here to represent the company and, as the guests would soon arrive, he needed them to be professional.

'From what I hear, you've seen it all before too,' Russell's friend muttered as he elbowed Naomi.

'Huh, just a drunken fumble at the welcome dinner,' she shrugged, but failed to hide her blush.

'Right, well the flight is arriving soon so we'll go over to arrivals in about ten minutes. Meanwhile, if you want to go to the toilet or get a drink or have a smoke outside, now is the time.'

Reps dispersed in every direction, some to do the things Mark had suggested, some to check their messages on the free airport wi-fi and some of the more nervous ones went to have another look around the departure lounge while they had the chance to take it all in.

Mark called his fiancée Zoe to see if she was ready for her first arrivals as she was waiting for them in the apartments of a mutual friend where she was working for the summer. He'd passed by that morning to find her painting the fence and worried that they were not up to speed with arrangements, but she reassured him everything was in place and it was just a little 'extra' that the owner had suggested. She confirmed that all the paintwork was dry and all the rooms were ready for occupation, inviting him to call in for a drink with her once the guests had been dropped off, and he agreed happily.

Fifteen minutes later he was gathering everyone together as the plane was about to land and he wanted them in place beforehand. As the arrivals hall was completely empty, there was a clear view through the tiny window out to the runway and a few of the reps actually got to see the plane arrive, while others saw the people carrier collect the passengers and deliver them to the Passport Control area.

Their arrivals lists had been prepared well in advance and the coach numbers for each accommodation were all written in and had been double checked with the drivers. Mark took a deep breath and appreciated the simplicity of the arrangement, because he knew this was the only time it would be so straightforward. For the rest of the season there would be some last-minute changes to accommodation, coach numbers and even coach drivers - sometimes it would happen even as the guests were coming through. It sounded horrific and occasionally it was, but mostly he got a real buzz from the excitement and rush of it all.

'OK, so is everyone ready?' he asked with a confident smile.

'Ready as we'll ever be,' Russell assured him.

The others smiled and nodded with a mixture of nerves and excitement.

'Look, I know we've had an intense fortnight of training and practising speeches and what-not, but you are allowed to enjoy it too,' he laughed. 'You all know what you're doing and how to do it and you're only here because you went through with all the applications, interviews and training sessions to do a job you're going to love in a place that you'll spend the best summer of your lives.'

'Amen.' Mark was for once surprised at Russell's brevity.

'These people have booked a holiday in the sun to enjoy some time out and to get away from it all and you are the first people to greet them as they step out and feel that unique Greek heat. All they need is for someone to acknowledge their effort and assure them they've made the right choice.'

'I can do that,' Naomi announced with determination.

'Good, and the rest of you?'

There were a few positive mumbles, but Mark could see lots of nods and smiles so he presumed he was on the right track.

'OK, well there's luggage coming through now, so

they'll be out any minute. Let's be professional now; we are representing the company as well as ourselves as individuals so if we show a united front, we'll make a brilliant first impression.'

'Yeah, baby. Let's do it. Teeth and tits,' Russell instructed as he struck up a pose which made everyone laugh, including Mark.

'Maybe smiles and a warm welcome are enough, thanks,' he nodded and took up his position as the first guests started to approach.

He was glad to see the laughter stayed on the reps' faces as all the guests exited the airport and made their way to the coaches which would take them on to their resort and their long-awaited holidays. He had a good feeling about this summer and hoped everyone would support each other through the more difficult airport transfers, delays and difficulties which were sure to occur as things got busier.

In the meantime he signed off all the reps' transfer lists to confirm that they had no missing passengers and then took a seat on Naomi's coach which was going to Kos Town and hoped she would deliver her arrival speech in the same genuine way she had surprised him with in the training process. It was going to be interesting to watch her development and he hoped she wouldn't get distracted by Russell again as she had at the pre-season bash. At least he was in Kardamena so there wasn't too much chance of them meeting each other in their free time.

He took another look at the airport as the coach pulled out and again realised that it was a different scenario, as he would usually have to wait until the plane had taken off, but with no guests on board he could leave with the other reps.

He sent a text message to Zoe to let her know he was on his way and he couldn't wait to celebrate the beginning of the season with her over a drink… or three!

.

MAY

Penelope gave Stelios a quick peck on the lips as they parted, secure in the knowledge that he would be watching her every step until she was out of sight. She also knew that out of sight was not out of mind as they were working the same shift, which didn't happen very often, so for the next eight hours he would be sitting downstairs to check the passengers through to the departure gates and she would be on the floor above serving them in the duty-free shop.

They had made the most of today's rota by spending the night together at his place, then getting ready for work and enjoying breakfast in the morning before she reminded him of her best assets and they had both needed another quick shower before rushing out to be in time for work. She was looking forward to the end of their shift too, as they had planned to go out for a meal and she was going to celebrate their six-month anniversary.

It was actually seven months since they had first started dating, but six months since they had been intimate together and as far as Penelope was concerned that had 'sealed the deal' for the future. She had been here before of course, thinking this was 'the one' like young women do, but it really did seem different this time.

Stelios was gorgeous, obviously. She wouldn't date a man who wasn't because part of her allure was that she knew she could get any man she wanted, and she didn't want an ugly one. She had no problem whatsoever attracting people (male and female) but unfortunately for them, most of them weren't what she considered suitable. She'd been involved with some very handsome men, but for one reason or another they hadn't worked out. One had been too dependent on his mother, another too wrapped up in his dog; in both cases she hadn't come first and that would never be acceptable. There had been the one who suddenly couldn't afford to go out or buy things, but when he started to ask for handouts she discovered he had a gambling problem so that had ended quickly. There had been the one who was very exciting and adventurous, but once that became obvious in the bedroom it all felt much too one-sided and she literally ran away. There were a couple who she hadn't been able to trust and one who had admitted from the beginning that he'd never be monogamous, so that was a no go for a relationship too. She'd also experienced an extremely passionate and intense fling while on holiday in Halkidiki, but resigned that to the 'holiday romance' file. She often recalled it during intimate moments when the person she was with wasn't really doing it for her, but never revealed it to anyone as it was the first and only time she had been with a woman. It was fine for a holiday fling, but she could never try anything like that on her home turf where people knew who she was.

So far, she had never needed to use those private moments to help with her current relationship, as Stelios could easily set her erogenous zones on fire simply by his expert touch. For all the other liaisons she'd had with men, no one had ever really managed to bring her to the point where she had completely surrendered and lost control, until Stelios. It was not the intense feeling she'd had with the Shakira lookalike, but it was passionate and satisfying so she couldn't imagine needing anything more for a successful relationship.

It wasn't all sex, of course, that was just the best bit. They both enjoyed good food and wine, so were often found at the top restaurants, savouring each mouthful and trying new dishes from as many countries as possible. Luckily, Penelope had what her mother called 'hollow legs' as she never seemed to put on weight and always stayed perfectly slim regardless of how calorific the sumptuous desserts were. Stelios loved to run, cycle and swim so he was always active enough to burn off those calories and tone up his muscles, which was definitely a plus point for Penelope. She sometimes tried to get him to pass on his run and 'work out' with her for some exercise instead, but he loved his schedule and often ran with friends so her persuasion didn't (usually) work, but she didn't stop trying as she wanted him all for herself eventually.

Penelope closed her locker and made her way to the checkout in the duty-free shop. Most days she worked as an advisor in the make-up and perfume section as that was her speciality, but there were only a couple of flights until lunchtime so just minimal staff and counter duties. She began by checking there were plenty of bags to carry the goods in. She hated that she had to ask every single time if they wanted a bag and tell them the price because, let's face it, who's buying bottles of vodka or whisky and not needing a bag? There were some, of course, and that was hilarious as they juggled everything while handing over their boarding card and trying to type their PIN number into the machine. Then they had to call over the husband or the child to assist with carrying the supersized box of biscuits, the 3 for 2 boxes of Turkish Delight, 2 bottles of olive oil and 4 jars of honey – one for each of the neighbours.

She picked up a few layers of tissue paper and tore them in half as they only came in one size which was far too big for some of the smaller souvenirs like shot glasses, mirrors and fridge magnets. She hoped they wouldn't sell too many small items this morning as it always played havoc with her nails on the sharp edges if she was rushing. She much preferred just talking about cosmetics and discussing shades of lipstick, or spritzing someone with a perfume sample without getting involved in who was jumping the queue, or where they should put the baskets when they'd finished, or cards getting declined, again. She didn't mind a casual chat about things that interested her, but she really couldn't be bothered with moaning travellers and ridiculous complaints.

At least she could dream about Stelios while she worked, knowing he was just downstairs and probably remembering the quick unexpected connection that morning with the same excitement as she did. She knew he couldn't get enough of her and that was exactly what she needed.

Mark stepped out to meet Naomi as she arrived with her departing passengers.

'Which desk number for the Manchester flight?'

'They haven't opened it yet so best not to give them a number, but probably 4 and 5. Just start a line from the end entrance door and queue them to the left, under cover.'

'Oh, am I the first to arrive?' she said as she bit her lower lip.

'Yes, but that's not a problem. You remember how we practised organising the queue?'

'Uh-huh.'

'So just do that and the others will be here in no time. Once everyone's here you can decide which parts of the queue you're looking after.'

'But can't I just take them in to start the line inside?' she asked with a shiver.

'No, not until I know for sure which desks they're using; it'll be horrendous if we have to move everyone around inside.'

'Mmm.' She didn't seem convinced.

'Look, I know it's windy and might even rain, but once the desk opens everyone will move forward quite a lot so it will seem like things are moving quickly. Now, just tell your guests what's going to happen before they make their own mind up,' he said, nodding behind her.

Naomi turned to see several people standing in the aisle of the coach and gradually moving forward in an attempt to be the first off and rush to check in, so she quickly hopped back on and picked up the microphone to let everyone know what was happening. Unfortunately, the gentleman who was most eager to get to the front of the queue was standing right opposite her at the top of the steps and not only heard the announcement through the speakers, but got the full force of her hot minty breath in his face. He gave her a look that was somewhere between disbelief and disgust, but she just smiled and wondered how he would have reacted if she hadn't had a few Tic Tacs to hide the smell of the garlic in the tzatziki she'd just had for lunch.

As she was organising the queue, she saw two more coaches arrive and was relieved that someone else would be able to take the lead, then suddenly blushed as she realised Russell was strolling over.

'Hey,' he smiled and somehow took her breath away.

'Er, hi,' she stammered her response.

'Didn't know you were going to be on this flight,' he smirked. 'Looks like this afternoon will be more fun than I thought.'

'Hmm,' she grinned and tried not to read too much into his flirtatious eye roll.

'My lot are just gonna join the queue, so I'll pop inside for a minute and check in with Mark.'

'Oh, right,' she nodded and then as soon as he was out of sight she smacked herself on the head with her clipboard. 'Idiot,' she murmured so her guests didn't overhear her admonish herself.

She could not understand how she had only managed to speak to Russell in words of one syllable, between shallow breaths. That wasn't her at all. She was more confident than that and she had proved it at the welcome dinner when they had performed 'Don't Go Breaking My Heart' – quite well, she thought – with the karaoke Mark had organised.

The free-flowing cocktails had certainly helped initially, but she had felt in control of their playful conversation and innuendoes until their drunken fumble behind the castle walls on the way to the nightclub, where she felt she had him in the palm of her hand. Quite literally.

For some reason she was now acting timid and distant and that was ridiculous so she decided to be less nervous and more approachable. Russell was a good-looking guy but they worked in different resorts and she was sure he had no shortage of willing female guests looking for a bit of fun, so she didn't need to consider him in that way. They could be good colleagues who enjoyed a bit of banter when they met, without all this stupid shyness and memories of personal intimacy.

'Penny for your thoughts,' Naomi heard in her right ear. Literally *in* her ear as Russell had approached silently and muttered the words so closely that she felt the hot air and moisture settle on her skin as distinctly as she could feel the snug fit of his body right behind hers. Instantly she felt goose bumps along her arm and if her hair hadn't been tied up in a ponytail it would be standing up on the back of her neck for anyone to see.

'Ooh, er... I'm just, er...' she faltered.

'Don't tell me,' he grinned as he moved to face her. 'You're deciding which karaoke song we can sing next time.'

'Next time?' Naomi was sure she was still using words of one syllable, but could not string her thoughts together. Next time for what? She could feel herself blush uncontrollably.

'Yeah. When the bar crawl gets going, I'll be bringing a coach up to Kos Town with my guests to share the evening and I know you do a bit of karaoke in one of the bars. We could make it a regular thing and choose something fun to get everyone going.'

'We could?'

'Sure, why not? It'll be a bit of fun and it can be *our thing*,' he winked.

'Our thing?'

'When you're selling the trips the billies always like to see the reps acting the fool and they go along just to see what an arse we make of ourselves,' he laughed. 'I don't mind if it's gonna make me more cash.'

'More cash,' she nodded.

'Hey, is there an echo in here? Why are you repeating everything I say? And don't say you're not.'

'I'm not,' she insisted, failing to see what was happening.

'OK, I'm guessing you've had a heavy night, so I'll come back once you've woken up. Better do it quick though, Mark picks up on that kind of thing really easy.'

'But,' Naomi began as Russell hurried down the line to keep his guests entertained.

Oh dear, this wouldn't do at all. Not only was she incapable of having a normal conversation with him, now he was going to be at the bar crawl every week with his seductive smile, worrying winks and luscious lips...

'No...' she moaned to herself as she realised that she fancied the most unreliable rep in the team.

'OK Naomi,' Mark called over. 'Send in the first forty or so people, making sure each party goes through together and I'll lead them to the check in at desks 3, 4 and 5. Once they're checking in I'll get one of the others to take over and let you know how many to send in each time.'

'Not Russell,' she gasped unexpectedly.

'No, not Russell. He's best outside with the waiting passengers. Why, is there a problem?'

'Oh, no, not at all. That's what I meant,' she stuttered breathlessly. 'He's better outside chatting to the guests.'

'OK,' Mark nodded uncertainly. That was a bit odd, but no time to investigate now. He would just have to keep an eye on things and see what the issue was between them. Hopefully just a little embarrassment over seeing each other again after their well-known 'secret' tryst. Well, better to get it out of the way now so they can continue the season without any further awkwardness, as they would be meeting all the time at the airport and on other guiding duties.

The first crowd of passengers rushed in but were quickly slowed by the zig zag effect of the check in area which allowed more people to queue in a confined space, but also required them to proceed at a sedate pace.

'Please make sure you have your passports ready along with your tickets or boarding cards for everyone in your party before you get to the check-in desk, to make things easier for the staff and quicker for yourselves. Thank you,' Mark instructed in a clear and authoritative voice.

He moved to the front of the queue and as people stepped away from the desk, he directed them to the scanner where they needed to put their cases and then on to the queue for passport control.

As soon as half a dozen groups had gone through and others could see what was happening, he stepped aside and the other rep took over, to say farewell to the guests and to liaise with Naomi to allow more passengers inside the building.

Around twenty minutes later Naomi asked to swap duties as she wanted some experience with the check-in procedure. The other rep was unsure as she thought they were supposed to stick to certain areas for clarity, but Naomi managed to sweet talk the nervous new Kefalos rep and made her way indoors. She failed to mention that it had started to rain outside and she was freezing, along with the fact that the waiting guests were all complaining to her as they passed by and she'd had enough. They weren't drenched as there was a small amount of coverage above the waiting area, but they were a bit damp as the wind had swept the wetness around somewhat and, of course, most of them were travelling home in shorts and flip flops which meant they were pretty cold too.

Everything went as planned with no unforeseen circumstances so Mark was pleased it had all gone smoothly and he'd had time to go through the arrivals paperwork and add the updates and coach numbers to each of the reps' lists.

Naomi was chatting to another Kos Town rep as the last guests were checked in and realised that she hadn't seen Russell since their strange conversation earlier. She glanced up and down the departure lounge but he was nowhere in sight. She wanted to go to the toilet but needed to tell Mark so that he didn't wonder where she'd disappeared to and went outside to where he was giving the coach drivers their instructions, to let him know.

He was deep in conversation and appeared to be in some kind of debate about who should drive to the all-inclusive hotels so she decided not to interrupt, after all, it wouldn't take long and she'd probably be back before he'd even noticed. As she turned away, she heard a high-pitched giggle and looked over to see the Kefalos rep leaning against the wall in the small alcove where reps and airport staff could almost unobtrusively have a quick cigarette break. She was slightly miffed that she'd been skiving while Naomi had been working hard, but immediately became infuriated when she realised that Russell was standing in front of her with his arm on the wall next to her face as he leaned in to tell her something supposedly amusing.

Did he have to be that close? What was he saying to her? Was she just pretending it was funny to impress him, or was it something much more suggestive?

All these questions were racing through her mind as she slipped on a small step before realising that she was marching straight towards them with a momentum that was difficult to adjust in order to redirect herself through the nearest door. She just about made it and escaped to the downstairs toilet.

She sat there for a while as she tried to get her breath under control. She couldn't understand why she'd reacted so badly over someone she wasn't even dating. They'd had one… what could she call it? An encounter? Too formal. A snog? But it was much more than that. An affair? No, it was much less than that. A mutual grope with lots of wet kisses? That was closer. A fling – that's all it was. They'd copped off and had a fling where they'd explored each other up close for an intense twenty minutes or so without any expectations of a repeat performance. So why the dramatic reaction to seeing him flirting with someone else? She needed a few minutes to gather her thoughts before she went back out there and had to face them again through the whole arrivals procedure. She really loved this job and didn't want to mess it up over some kind of crush for an unsuitable bloke. She heard the door open and decided to wait until whoever it was had gone before leaving her cubicle to reapply her make-up for extra confidence.

'I know, seriously, you'd think they'd at least bring a jacket. I'm sure one of the blokes was wearing a onesie to fly home in,' the unidentified voice laughed.

'And just where did they think we were going to get umbrellas from?' her friend added.

'Though to be honest, I was freezing my bits off out there. Looked like Russell was keeping you warm though.'

Naomi's ears ached as she realised it was her fellow Kos Town rep talking to the Kefalos rep she had run in there to avoid.

'What? No way. He's just a chancer.'

'Bloody good-looking chancer though and, from what I've heard, pretty good in the sack too!'

'From what you've heard?'

Naomi tried to suss out if that sounded like a twinge of jealousy, or interest?

'Well, he was here last year, wasn't he? Some of the other reps have let it be known he was quite the lothario.'

Naomi cringed as she realised that each of the girls had taken a cubicle either side of hers. What were the chances?

'Well, exactly. I'm not about to become another notch on his bedpost. He's not my type anyway.'

'Probably just as well, I think he's got something going on with Naomi.'

'No, I think that was just gossip. He said they got too drunk and had a bit of a snog, but it was a mistake and they're just friends now.'

Naomi felt her stomach thud as though it was about to empty suddenly, but she couldn't quite work out

28

which way it was going to go.

'Oh really? I thought they quite liked each other. I guess they're in different resorts though, so they won't get to see each other much.'

Naomi was initially happy that someone had spotted their mutual attraction, but then worried that she was wearing her heart on her sleeve and that was never a good thing. At the same time, she started to feel hot and sweaty which meant she was probably going to throw up sometime soon.

'But we get to meet up all the time at the airport and guiding and days off...'

'Yeah, but I mean on a one to one basis. You can't have a relationship while you're at work and there's not really enough time to get together outside of that unless you're in the same resort.'

'Hmm, I guess so,' the Kefalos rep admitted with what sounded like a hint of regret to Naomi.

There followed a moment of silence followed by two flushes and some hand washing in the area opposite.

'That lipstick looks great on you. It's... playful.'

'Oh, I've worn it for years; it makes me feel in control.'

'Well, you want to be careful. The way Russell's hanging on to you today, he might want you to take control of *him*.'

'I doubt there's a woman alive who could control him,' the Kefalos rep laughed as they moved towards the exit.

'Oh, you could give it a go,' she heard as the door closed behind them.

What Naomi would have given to have heard the next couple of sentences in that conversation, but she didn't have time to think about it as her lunch made a sudden reappearance and she had to freshen up before she could face them all again.

Mark was pacing up and down and shouting into his phone as she took her place to greet the guests, thankful that the rain, if not the wind, had finally given up.

'Yes, two more taxis. I've just got an email notification of four extra passengers but the coaches are full and they won't fit into one taxi with luggage. Sorry, I didn't get that...'

He turned round quickly and knocked into Naomi.

'Sorry, I can't hear a word, he sounds like he's in a wind tunnel. Yes, Elias, I'm here. Just text me with the details. The flight's here now but the luggage hasn't arrived yet. Thanks.'

'Sounds tricky,' she offered.

'Yeah, but I'm getting it sorted. Are you ok? You look a bit pale.'

'Fine, just that time, you know?' Always a sure-fire way of avoiding unwanted attention.

'Oh, yeah, right. Listen, why don't you organise the taxis? You can sit at the desk there and just check people into the right taxis as we send them over. We need another two but they're on their way now so it won't be too difficult to manage. How's that?' he asked with a genuine smile.

'That sounds good, thanks.'

She made her way over to the taxi rank where she confirmed who was going where and took a seat until she was needed. She'd forgotten that Mark had a fiancée and was probably used to time of the month problems so she felt bad that she'd used it as an excuse, but glad that it got her out of the way while she was feeling nauseous for a different reason.

She would definitely have to work out what was going on in her head when she thought about Russell because it was clearly not wise to get mixed up with him. She knew she would be able to see the logical side and understand it was better to stay away from him, she just didn't know where she would find the strength she was going to need when she was close to him and he was turning on that irresistible charm.

Smaragda made herself an instant coffee with lots of milk and sugar, using the canteen kettle which had definitely seen better days. She needed a hot caffeine hit after checking in the noisy Brits for their flight as it was unusually cold and they had tried her patience.

She smiled to herself as she recalled some of the conversations she'd overheard and the fact that each nationality had its own priorities. Brits always argued over who was sitting with the kids, Germans wanted extra leg room, Swedes wanted window seats, the Dutch preferred to sit at the back and the Greeks just wanted to sit near the toilets.

After they had all checked in, the manifest showed an extra passenger had been issued with a boarding pass compared to the number they had expected, so it took some time to work out what had happened and find a solution. In the end, it wasn't too drastic for the passenger as it was an infant who had been issued with a seat when they were supposed to sit on a guardian's lap, but the flight wasn't full and the adjacent seat was empty anyway. It just required the cabin staff to point out the mistake and ensure the party was seated correctly for take-off, with the understanding they were able to use the extra seat once they were in the air.

Unfortunately, for the staff member who had made the mistake it wasn't so simple. Smaragda had to issue an official warning and make sure the girl understood what she had done wrong. She would be on office duty until she had undertaken a refresher course and work with supervision for the following three check-in schedules. It seemed a bit over the top to the other staff, but she was just following the rules as the new fully automated system was not yet in place and each individual entry had to be approved personally. Any mistake on a flight manifest was a big deal and, not only the staff, but the airport itself could face charges or investigation for more serious errors and that had to be avoided at all costs.

She held the cup up to her lips as she blew the steam away, enjoying the warming sensation through the palms of her hands. She was just wondering if she could be bothered to get up and find some biscuits or cake in the fridge when Stelios came in and gave her a wave.

'Oh, see if there are any biscuits or something sweet around,' she called over.

'And I'm not sweet enough?' he asked with that familiar smile.

'Huh, funny,' she nodded sarcastically. 'Something with chocolate would be good.'

'Mmm. Now you're talking.' He put the kettle on again and had a look around the counter tops.

'Try the fridge,' she suggested.

'Won't they belong to someone else?' he asked with a frown.

'Maybe, but they're always stealing my stuff and if there's a few to choose from they might not notice.'

Stelios raised his eyebrows and cautiously opened the fridge door. There was a cling-film-covered plate of half-eaten moussaka, some stuffed vine leaves, a few tubs with names on, a solid lump of cake left over from the opening day celebration six weeks earlier and several different sandwiches in an assortment of wrappings.

'No luck, I'm afraid,' he said with relief, as he closed the fridge door to remove the unpleasant sight from his eyes.

'Seriously? Oh, I could really do with a chocolate fix,' she said dreamily as she licked her lips in anticipation.

'OK, wait there,' he instructed.

'Like I've got anywhere else to go...' she said to his back as he left the room.

She hoped he was going in search of some sweet goodies as she really did need a bit of a lift before she went back to continue her shift. There was a Russian flight to organise later and she knew she would need to be on top form for that as they almost always went over the weight limit for their luggage and pretended not to understand the rules to avoid paying extra.

She knew she could rely on Stelios to look after her, he always had. Except for the time he fell off his bike doing a wheelie and she had looked after him while his broken leg healed. Well, his mum helped a bit, but she was the buddy he'd turned to for entertainment and reassurances that he would be back and better than ever in no time. They had watched TV together through that summer and read all the superhero comics they could get their hands on. She never regretted staying by his side and missing out on the parties and days out the other kids were enjoying; they wouldn't have been the same without Stelios so she didn't want to waste her time and she didn't want him to suffer on his own. They'd made a great team then and they still did now, both finding jobs at the airport; it seemed perfectly natural for them to spend loads of time together as they always had done and, she presumed, they always would.

'Ta da!' Stelios announced as he returned, waving a couple of chocolate bars in the air, which he had obviously obtained from the vending machine.

'Yes!' Smaragda said, pumping her fist with satisfaction.

He placed them on the table as he brewed his green

tea and then sat opposite her as she wolfed down the first bar.

'So, didn't you get anything for yourself?' she asked in surprise.

'Oh, well, er...'

'Hmm. I thought you would've picked up something too,' she shrugged as she picked up the second bar.

'I, er, had a big lunch?' he said in explanation.

'Oh, I see,' she replied with a smile, toying with the wrapper. 'So, you don't need any more treats this afternoon?'

'No, I'm good,' he replied with resignation.

'Ha, every time,' she laughed. 'You fall for it every time.' She shook her head as she pushed the second chocolate bar back across the table towards him.

'Oh, what?' he declared, placing his hand on his chest in fake surprise. 'You mean, you're not going to eat both of them?'

'Of course not, silly. I'm just teasing, but it looks like you've sussed my methods by now.'

'I know you too well, sister. And just to prove it, I did buy that one for you.' He pushed the treat back across the table to her. 'And I got myself a flapjack, which hopefully hasn't broken down into crumbs in my pocket.'

He pulled out the packet and was happy to find it still all in one piece.

'Oh, I see,' she said rather deflated. 'I'm that predictable.'

'Not always. You can still surprise me sometimes.' He suddenly had an unexpected memory of how grown up she had looked at the end-of-school formal, years ago.

'And you surprise me, too.' She was always surprised with his occasional flippant referral to her as 'sister' as she felt uncomfortable being thought of that way. She supposed it was a compliment, but somehow it just never felt right.

'We make a good team, then,' he winked and touched his cup against hers in a mark of solidarity and celebration.

'Yes, that's true,' she nodded as she tried to dismiss that awkward feeling of nervousness as their fingers touched briefly.

'Hey, did you check-in that woman with purple hair? She was a complete lunatic! She had her hands full at the passport office and dumped everything along the sill while she handed it over. Then, she started packing things away while I was trying to get eye contact to approve the ID and told me to 'hang on' while she sorted out her bag!'

'No, she didn't check-in with me, but I did see her. I think she was a bit tiddly.'

'You can say that again. Eventually I tried to hand her passport back, but she wouldn't take it until I'd told her which shade of lipstick I preferred from the little plastic bag she had her liquids in.'

'What?' Smaragda laughed as she could imagine the look of horror on Stelios' face.

'I know. Like I'm supposed to know what shade of lipstick is best. Like it matters,' he shrugged. 'Who's looking anyway?'

'That must have been funny to watch, though. After you got over the surprise,' she added.

'Not really, but I solved it in a more diplomatic way than the way she was suggesting...' he paused.

'Which was...?' Smaragda's interest was piqued.

'She suggested trying both and kissing me on each cheek to see which shade suited my skin best.'

Smaragda found the look of dismay on his face fascinating as it was an expression she wasn't sure she'd seen before. She opened her mouth to comment, but found she didn't want to break the spell.

'So how did I solve it, I hear you ask?' he continued with raised eyebrows, prompting her to nod with what she hoped looked like eagerness.

'I told her to visit Penelope in the duty-free shop for the best advice and say that Stelios had sent her so that if she wanted to buy anything, she could get ten percent off.'

He sat back, awaiting praise and adulation for getting out of an awkward situation, while possibly increasing his girlfriend's commission figures.

'Well, I'm sure she appreciated it,' was all Smaragda could manage.

'Who, the lady with the purple hair, or Penelope?'

'Both, probably,' she shrugged.

Smaragda tore open the packet of the second chocolate bar which she had been intending to save for later and gorged on the sweetness to lift her spirits. Penelope was fairly new on the scene and Smaragda always felt insignificant when she pictured the perfect princess in all her glory with flawless skin, glossy hair, impeccable manicure and sensational figure. She had never been anything other than pleasant to Smaragda, but she just didn't seem like the right fit for Stelios and she was finding it difficult to keep her opinions to herself.

'Well, hopefully Penny will appreciate it later,' he sighed and Smaragda noticed how the smile didn't quite reach his eyes. She preferred his smile when they'd shared an amusing moment, making his whole face light up and allowing his soft and succulent lips to reveal slightly uneven, but perfectly natural, teeth.

'I'm sure she appreciates everything you do for her,' she replied, with more emphasis than she had intended. 'Especially if you bring her lots of chocolate goodies like this,' she added as she enjoyed the last mouthful with a wink.

'No, that's just my buddy's treat. Can't have you fading away on me now, can I?' he said as he reached over and placed his hand on her arm in a show of camaraderie.

'Oh, that'll never happen,' she laughed nervously as she stood and moved to wash her cup. 'Too much flab on these thighs to disappear overnight.'

'Don't be daft,' he laughed. 'There's nothing wrong with your thighs. When we go out running, they're super fit and strong.'

'Yeah? Well, they are getting better, but I'd prefer it if they'd stop wobbling. See you later,' she said as she quickly left before the astonishment of knowing Stelios had been looking at her thighs registered on her face and gave away her confusion.

'OK, have a good afternoon,' he replied as she suddenly disappeared.

He hoped he hadn't offended her. He knew she had an issue with her weight but she wasn't fat by any means. She'd always reminded him of a pared-down chunky Jennifer Lopez, without the make-up, teased hair and fancy clothes, but looking better for it. All she needed was to tone up her muscles a little and she would hopefully regain some of that confidence she'd had at school where she believed she could do anything. She had seemed to quietly disappear into herself recently but he knew he could help her - with a regular running routine to give her a purpose - to find that love of life again and maybe even to find someone to share it with. He would be so delighted if she could be as happy and loved as she deserved to be.

JUNE

Mark parked the car and strolled over to the terminal, enjoying the warm sunshine and looking forward to what the weather forecast had described as a 'mini heatwave' the next weekend.

He loved those baking hot days for which Greece was famous and couldn't wait to top up his healthy tan for something deeper and more lasting. He'd been repping a good few years and had started to get a bit tired of the same procedures, the same trips to guide and the same complaints, but he would never get tired of the beautiful Greek countryside, small friendly villages and the stunning beaches where he would spend all his free time when he could.

For the moment he was making the most of how well he knew the system, which made his job a lot easier to deal with as he could do his airport and guiding duties on autopilot and have stock responses to unjustified complaints, as well as having gained enough experience to give him the confidence to deal with any new and unexpected issues.

He spotted his friend Pantelis, who had a small car hire shop in Kos Town and who had helped him out a lot in the past when he'd sold his cars instead of the more established names. When he'd only had a moped to get around on, he'd often been able to get a 'freebie' on his day off so he could go down to Kardamena or Kefalos, which wouldn't have been possible if he'd stuck to the company he was supposed to advertise. Luckily, no one had ever discovered his duplicity and the friendship had stayed firm and still included the odd perk.

'Hey, how's it going?' Mark shouted over the tops of the cars.

'Good. How's you?'

'I'm doing OK. Another airport day so I'll be busy with back to back flights.'

'Ela tho,' Pantelis called him to come over with an exaggerated wave.

Mark had a feeling he knew where this conversation was heading.

'You don't sell many cars now. What happened?'

There it was.

'I'm the Head Rep now Pantelis, so I'm more of a supervisor and I only visit one hotel.'

'It's a big hotel though, eh? One of those Ayy Iyy ones?'

Mark had to smile. The way Pantelis pronounced the initials for All Inclusive made it seem much more other-worldly and more like he was referring to Artificial Intelligence.

'Yes, but it's so far out of town, near the Thermal Springs, that the people who stay there have usually booked a get-away-from-it-all break and don't want to go touring around.'

'But you can tweet talk them, yes?'

'I don't know... Oh, you mean sweet talk them?'

'That's what I said,' Pantelis replied with a frown.

'Well, I try my best. It works sometimes; I had a few bookings last week.'

'A few, yes. But you always sell more than this in another summer.'

'I'm sorry, pal. I will try harder, but I'm only getting about ten percent of my arrivals from last year.'

'Hmm. What about the other reps?'

Mark was slightly winded by the elbow which had just punched his ribs.

'Oh, well, they have to use the company they've been given the paperwork for I'm afraid. And I just don't think the reps who've taken over the hotels I used to work in are clever enough to pull it off like I did.'

'Pull it off?'

'I mean, I don't think they would be able to use both companies at once without getting mixed up who was booked with who?'

'They stupid?' Pantelis asked, but was already nodding in answer to his own question.

'They just wouldn't know how to do it without being found out, then everyone would be in trouble.'

'Hmm. No trouble,' he agreed.

'Tell you what, though,' Mark suggested. 'Zoe already has information for your services at the Irini apartments, where she's working, if anyone asks while the rep isn't there.'

'Yes, good girl. She has sold one or two.'

'Well, if you could do some kind of special offer just for them, above the usual ones, she might be able to send more customers your way.'

'But I am giving free days and low rates now. You want me to drive them around like a taxi?'

'No, not at all. Let me think…'

'I can't go lower price. I have to cut under the big boys.'

'I know that. I'm trying to think of something you could offer without costing too much.'

'It all costs too much unless they hire for many days.'

'OK, what about this? If they book the car for a minimum of 5, 6 or 7 days, you give them a full tank of petrol?'

'I always give a full tank of petrol, that is normal.'

'Yes, but then you ask them to fill it again before they return it.'

'Of course, but sometimes they do not and I have problems.'

'I know, I've been involved in some of those cases. No, what I mean is, give them a full tank and then say if they book over a certain amount of days, they don't have to fill it up again. It's a bargaining tool which might work.'

'But that is many euros to give.'

'Yes, if you're talking a full tank. But how many people are likely to completely empty the tank anyway? OK, some might do it to get the whole benefit, but mostly they'll just use what they need and not worry if there's any left so you wouldn't have to fill a full tank each time.'

'Still, they will use most of it so it will be many euros.'

'But if you've rented it for a week or so, you'll make your profit on that and, anyway, over that period of time they will probably have to fill up in-between anyway and you might even get half a tank back.'

'I don't know, Mark. I will have to work out if it is possible.'

'That's good. You work out the figures and let me know if it's something you can offer. It would only be for the ones at Irini, so it's not like every customer would expect it and it might tempt them to hire from you if they know they're getting a special deal that no one else is.'

'OK, I will think.'

'You do that. Now I need to go and organise the first of these flights.' He held his hand out to shake Pantelis' and to put an end to the conversation.

'Oh, Mark,' Pantelis said as he held onto the hand, refusing to miss an opportunity. 'This car is dropped here today and is now free. I am taking it back to the office, but I can leave here if you can sell for me to your new guests?'

'Sorry, my friend. I am working in departures today,' he lied. 'I won't see any arriving guests and probably they will be too tired and not safe to drive straight away anyway.'

'Hmm,' Pantelis grinned. 'Worth a try.'

'Always worth a try, old pal. Let's try the petrol thing and see if we can make things better for you.'

He gave Pantelis a farewell salute and turned to start his long day as airport controller, keeping his fingers crossed for everything to be on time.

Smaragda was just tucking into her lunch as Stelios came rushing in.

'Oh, thank goodness you're here,' he said breathlessly as he dropped onto the chair beside her.

'Whatever's wrong? Is it auntie?' She was concerned for his mother as she'd been suffering with a bad cold which had settled on her chest.

'No, she's OK, don't worry. She actually told me off for buying her some flowers yesterday, so I think she's feeling better.'

'Oh, thank heavens,' she sighed with relief.

'I've got a more urgent problem right now.'

'Oh?' *What could be more urgent than family's health?*

'Yes, it's Penelope.'

'I see.' Of course.

'It's her birthday tomorrow and I was going to buy some flowers and chocolates and then we were just on the phone now and I stupidly said I had a nice surprise for tomorrow.'

'Hmm. Well I guess flowers and chocolates are probably not her kind of surprise.'

'Exactly. She said that she loved surprises as most blokes could only be bothered to get some fancy flowers and cheap chocolates. Now she is expecting something out of this world because she said I was in a different class and would stop at nothing to give her the perfect treat.'

'Really?' Smaragda desperately tried to hide the smirk which wouldn't quit, as Stelios was the most down to earth guy she knew. He was nowhere near a 'different class' and wouldn't have a clue how to pretend to be that kind of person.

'Yes, I know, very funny. What am I going to do? It's

far too late to try to organise anything now.'

'Well it is if you're trying to plan something out of this world, but if you just want something special you could get a fancy necklace or earrings. I would think she'd like a shiny trinket.'

'Mmm. Jewellery. That might work.'

'Not jewellery, like from a jewellers. That would cost a fortune.' And give her ideas.

'But she'd never wear anything tacky. Or silver. It would have to be gold. And probably with a diamond, or at least a gemstone...'

'OK, let's think of something else more suitable.' It was only a matter of time before he decided to buy a big glitzy ring and he would be the only one who would think it was a fashion item.

'That might be a good idea though. I just wish I could remember what kind of jewellery she usually wears...'

Smaragda wondered how he didn't know that Penelope always had a gold chain with the letter P round her neck and a pair of small diamond earrings. She had a lightweight charm bracelet and an old-fashioned diamond ring which looked like an heirloom on one hand, with a large amethyst ring on the other. That was just for work, so presumably she would have more dressy items for going out and had probably been wearing some special pieces for her dates with Stelios, which he obviously hadn't noticed. What had he been looking at? Oh, yes. Those.

'What about some perfume? She must have a favourite out of all those that she sells every day?'

'Has she? But then she gets a good discount on it herself so that wouldn't be anything out of the ordinary.'

'So I guess make-up is out as well?'

'Yeah, it's like a necessity for her, not a treat.'

'She must have told you some of the things she enjoys. Can't you remember when she's talked about something that she's been excited about?'

'I don't know. Oh!' His eyes popped open, then he quickly turned away as it seemed he was trying to hide something. Was he blushing?

'Go on, you've obviously remembered something.' She was scared to ask, but really needed to know what had prompted that reaction. Or did she?

'Oh, it's nothing. Just something I remembered but it's not relevant.'

'Try me.'

'No, it's not something I can really... It doesn't matter.'

'Is it something she would like?'

'Hell, yeah,' he nodded eagerly. Smaragda felt as though he had punched her in the stomach but couldn't understand why the fact that he shared a personal secret with his girlfriend would hurt so much.

'Look, I'm your oldest friend. You can tell me.' *Please don't tell me*.

'Well, I don't know. We've never really discussed... I don't know how to...'

'It's me, Stelios. We can talk about anything and everything. We always have.' *Until now*.

'Well, OK. You're a girl so you can probably help me out a bit.'

'I'm glad you noticed,' she laughed unconvincingly.

'Just when we, er...' He searched for the right words. The least descriptive words. 'When we're *together*, she likes to wear certain... special... Oh, I can't say this.'

'You're into bondage?' Smaragda hissed with horror at the thought. Then she was filled with even more horror that she'd actually just said those words out loud in front of Stelios.

'No, are you crazy? Nothing like that. As if!' he added, to make a point.

'Then what is it she likes to wear? Fancy dress?' She knew she was feeling on edge, which made her go into defensive mode and appear rude, but she hadn't expected this conversation when she had started her lunch break and it was becoming unpleasantly uncomfortable.

Stelios stared at her as though she had thrown the worst kind of abuse at him, then two seconds later burst into fits of laughter.

'Oh, you are so funny,' he gulped. 'That's hilarious… Ha ha, fancy dress!'

Smaragda was suddenly wrenched out of her anxiety by the uplifting sight of Stelios, so completely happy and transformed by something she had inadvertently said in the heat of the moment.

'You'll be getting laughter lines if you carry on like that,' she smiled, though she couldn't imagine anything more lovely.

'It'll be your fault,' he sniffed as he took control again. 'I love how you can make me laugh.'

'That's what I'm here for,' she shrugged, accepting the compliment with pleasure.

'You're always here for me. I see that now. I don't know why I was so nervous to say what I was thinking when it's really quite straightforward.'

'You don't have to,' she reassured him, not even sure she wanted him to reveal his secret, now they'd shared a laugh together and replaced awkwardness with affection.

'It's underwear. Plain and simple. Well, obviously not

plain and simple in Penny's case. She likes to wear lacy, racy underwear.'

'Ah. I see.' Of course she would. With a perfect figure like hers, why wouldn't she want to decorate it to show it off?

'Yeah. She likes white for work, but on a date night she likes red, animal print or black.' His eyes glazed over and Smaragda tried not to picture the scene the way he presumably was.

'Are you sure she likes to wear it? Or maybe she just likes to wear it for you?' This was difficult for Smaragda to say, they had never discussed the mechanics of either of them having a relationship, but there was a reason for the question. A good one.

'Well, she says she loves wearing it because it makes her feel sexy.'

Smaragda squirmed.

'Though she has also said she loves how I look at her when she's wearing it… And how she gets turned on when I slowly peel it off her…' He was miles away and Smaragda could only presume he was so caught up in the image that he'd forgotten it was her he was speaking to.

'That was what I was thinking. I've never actually done it before, so I can't guarantee I'm right, but I have read in magazines that girls always buy… fancy underwear,' she wanted to say 'sexy' but couldn't manage that in Stelios' presence, 'to impress their men. It's usually for the guy's benefit rather than their own.'

'Yeah, I can see that,' he smiled, obviously still lost in the vision and not really hearing what she was saying.

'Stelios. You can't buy Penelope a gift of underwear for her birthday when she wears it as a gift for you. You'd be buying yourself the present.'

49

'Huh? Oh… Yeah, I get it,' he said glumly as the apparition and the idea was swept aside.

'Look, let's take this out of the bedroom as whatever you do there can be a gift I don't need to know about.' She made that comment with determination, hoping that she would never have to hear about (or imagine) his private life again.

'If we must,' he smirked, glad to have got over the awkwardness with Smaragda and thankful they were now in a place where he could discuss things like that with her openly without worrying about her reaction.

'What would you normally do? Where would you normally go on a date?'

'Hmm. We go to the beach in the daytime, maybe down on the south coast for a special treat.'

'But aren't you working tomorrow?'

'Yeah, how did you know?'

'I saw it on the rota when I checked my hours.' *Plus, I always like to know if you'll be here*.

'I tried to swap it so we could both be off, but there was no chance. Penelope's going to have a lazy day with her mum, then we're going out at night.'

'So a day trip is no use. We're thinking of something you like to do at night… In the evening,' she corrected herself before they went down the same road again.

'All the usual stuff; we go to the cinema, go for drinks at the Omega Sky Bar, stroll around the harbour, do a bit of clothes shopping and then always end up at one of our favourite restaurants.'

'Oh, what about a sunset cruise? You can get a nice champagne supper and it's warm enough in the evenings now.'

'No can do with the boat. Apparently, she can't get on a boat without throwing up.'

'There's such a thing as seasickness pills,' she reminded him with incredulity.

'I suggested that when I wanted to go over to Nissyros, but she absolutely refused. I think she may just be scared of the water because she never goes for a swim either, but she's never admitted as much.'

'Oh. That's unusual.' She meant it was unusual that Penelope couldn't be honest with Stelios if they were in a committed relationship, but she knew he would take it to mean being scared of the water and that was probably the easier option.

'I know, it puts a bit of a spanner in the works for romantic boat trips. Or even normal days out,' he replied with what seemed like a hint of annoyance.

'So, what else have we got. You like going out for meals. Is there a place you've been dying to go and haven't got there yet?'

'I don't think so…' Stelios rubbed his chin as he thought about some of the local restaurants. 'I think we've pretty much been to every worthwhile restaurant in town.'

'Only in town? What about out of town?'

'We both like wine with our meals, so we always get a taxi and tend to stay local.'

'But you've been out on dates to other villages?' She was thinking of her favourite place and couldn't imagine not being able to go there due to drinking or taxi issues.

'We did at first, but when she's had a drink, she gets a bit… frisky,' he laughed. 'One taxi driver saw much more than he bargained for when we were coming back from Tingaki one night so it's better if we can get back home quickly before the passion takes over.'

'Right,' Smaragda observed through clenched teeth. Back to *that* again.

'But neither of us are working the next day, so I guess we could stay over somewhere… Make a night of it?'

'I suppose it depends how much you want to spend? Bearing in mind you were initially thinking flowers and chocolates,' she reminded him with raised eyebrows.

'That's never going to work. I'll need to flex the plastic if I'm going to give her the birthday she's imagining.'

'OK. I've got an idea but depending on your budget it can be split into three so you can choose how much you want to spend and how big a deal you want to make it.'

'Brilliant! What's the plan?'

'Not so fast Romeo. I need to find out if the places are open and if they can do what I'm thinking of. Then I'll get some prices and get back to you. My lunch hour is almost over, so I'll have a look on my afternoon break and email you with details later.'

'I knew there was a reason you were my best friend,' Stelios said as he gave her a hug before he left.

'Smaragda saves the day again,' she said to herself as she thought over her plans for Penelope's birthday. It was something she'd always wanted to do for herself, but without anyone to share it with, it wouldn't feel as special as it should. If she couldn't have it for herself, she wanted to give it to Stelios and hoped that somehow he would enjoy it for both of them.

Mark knew his phone was ringing as he had made sure it was on vibrate because the airport was so packed he would've had no chance to hear it. He fished it out of his pocket and noticed the call was from one of the Tingaki reps who was on a departure transfer, so he made his way outside, hoping it would be at least slightly quieter out there.

'Hello, this is Mark. Can you hear me?'

'Yes, I can hear you fine.'

'Hang on, I'll just go towards arrivals where it's quieter; I can't properly hear you.'

It was one thing to have the most up to date telephone technology, but totally useless inside a busy airport and Mark was used to having to sprint away from the crowds when the transfer reps called.

'OK, that should be better. What's up?'

'I've done my pick-ups in Tingaki and Marmari but they took longer than planned because there was a dispute in one hotel over the bill.'

'Are you OK? You sound out of breath,' he asked with concern.

'I'm fine, just walking. Anyway, I got to Mastichari harbour to pick up the passengers who'd come over from Kalymnos and I'm missing two people.'

'Oh crap.'

'Yeah, tell me about it. They're not in the restaurant we use as a meeting place and I can't see any extra luggage. I'm just checking out the other cafés in case they've gone to the wrong one, but can you contact the ferry people and check if they actually came over while I look?'

'No worries, I'll call you back in a few minutes.'

Of course, he had no paperwork with him so he had to run back to departures to pick up his contact list, check everything was still under control with the Birmingham check-in, then back out to call the office in Kalymnos who had transported the passengers over from the sponge divers island that morning. Luckily, they answered first time and had all the information so without delay he was back on the phone.

'Hi, yes, they definitely came over on the ferry. Are you sure their luggage isn't there?'

'There wasn't anything left after all the others boarded the coach so I was thinking they didn't come over, but I'm in another café now and there are two cases here.'

'Oh, right. Have you checked the luggage tags?'

'Guess what? There aren't any! Just let me speak to the waiter...'

Mark heard her ask if he knew where the people who left the cases might be, but he didn't know anything about it. She asked if anyone else was working there and he went to get the manager.

'Just checking out if anyone knows who these cases belong to. How am I doing for time? I know I'm on the late side after the hassle at the Marmari hotel.'

'Well the other reps are here and checking in, so you're the last one, but it'll only take ten minutes from there so you're OK for a little while.'

'Hang on...'

Again, she asked someone about the cases and he heard a longer reply but couldn't quite make out what was going on.

'Well, an older couple did buy some soft drinks in bottles and asked if they could leave their cases while they had a stroll on the beach, so it could be them.'

'Maybe, but how long have you been away from the coach now?'

'About ten minutes.'

'With the earlier delay and another ten minutes, that's really not good for the people you picked up in Tingaki so you can't really hang around much longer.'

'I know, but if they're close to here, I need to have a little look.'

'Can you leave a note on their cases, quickly, to say what's happened?'

'Yes, I will. I'll just go around the front of the café to the beach side and make sure they're not just sitting there… Oh, WOW! Ow!' She shouted down the phone as some kind of foghorn blew very loudly and very close by.

'What the hell was that?' Mark asked as soon as it stopped, though his ear was pounding and he only very tentatively replaced the phone against it in case it began again.

'It was the owner ringing a hideous alarm and now EVERYONE is looking at us!'

Mark heard some commotion in the background and could make out that the rep was talking to some people who had obviously gathered to find out what was happening.

'Mark, I'll call you back in a couple of minutes.'

'OK, but you need to get back to the coach before the passengers…' but she had cut the line.

He hoped she wasn't now getting involved in a local dispute over the disturbance at the café. She did have time to get to the airport and check-in, but he didn't want her to get distracted with something else and be on the last minute as that wasn't good for the guests and would give him less time to organise things in the arrivals afterwards.

He made his way back to the doorway of the

departures and could see there was no queue outside and all the passengers were now in the zig zag formation in front of the check-in desks, so they would be through by the time she did arrive.

His thoughts were interrupted by the Kefalos rep who was approaching with a sheepish expression.

'Mark, I've just been talking to Russell and he's thinking of spending his day off next week in Kefalos to do some windsurfing.'

'Oh, OK.' He remembered Russell was into sports and he knew that in Kastri Bay on the Kefalos coast it was ideal for harnessing the wind in that way. He'd done it himself in the past, but he was hoping he wasn't being invited to join him this time. But, in that case, why wasn't Russell himself asking?

'I just wondered, if he came down the night before after duties, could I book him into one of my guaranteed units that has a spare room?'

'Er, yeah. If he wants to,' Mark shrugged. It was one of the perks for the reps to stay occasionally in an apartment unit which had already been contracted and paid for the season, if there were any spare rooms. It wasn't a big deal, but they did have to ask for permission, so he was pleased they weren't taking advantage.

'Great, thanks,' she said as she returned indoors, though her grateful smile seemed to express more happiness than he'd expected for such a simple request.

His phone rang again and he answered it instantly.

'Well, all's well that ends well,' the Tingaki rep told him.

'You've found them?' he asked with his fingers crossed.

'Yep. They'd gone to a different café as the lady

didn't like the smell of fish from the main restaurant on the harbour front. They'd bought some drinks and sat on an empty sunbed while they had them, but then fell asleep and missed their pick up time. They just woke up when they heard the siren that the owner set off to attract attention and realised they were late.'

'So they're on the coach now?'

'We're just walking there now, but the lovely waiters from the café have gone ahead with their cases so it won't be long before we set off.'

'OK, that's good. Don't forget to apologise for keeping them waiting on the coach.'

'Will do. What did you say in the training course? Tell them I just wanted to give them a chance to enjoy Kos for a little longer before they had to leave?'

'That's it. I'm surprised you remembered,' he said with a mixture of pride and pleasure.

'Oh, it really had an effect on me and I thought how much I'd enjoy hearing it myself, so it stuck in my mind. Hopefully I won't have to use it too many times though.'

'Yeah, hopefully. OK, the queue is almost through here so just tell them to come straight in to desks one and two and we'll be waiting for you.'

'Great, thanks Mark.'

'No worries, see you soon.'

It wasn't the first time there had been problems with the pick up at Mastichari harbour and it wouldn't be the last, but he was glad this issue had been resolved, even if it had left his head pounding from that noisy foghorn!

Stelios parked the car outside the house and straightened his shirt, tie and suit as he walked up to the door, with a final swipe back of his hair at the temples before he knocked.

'Why is he knocking? Just tell him to come in!' Penelope's mother called loud enough for him to hear.

'Hello handsome,' Penelope murmured with admiration as she opened the door to a preened and prepared Stelios.

'Hah… er, hi,' Stelios stammered as the vision of perfection in front of him stepped back to allow him to enter.

'Come in, come in, let me look at you,' her mother instructed urgently.

'Here I am,' he said with a smile as he greeted her. 'This is for you.' He handed her a single white rose bud which was ready to burst open at any moment.

'Oh, how lovely. You see, my daughter, anyone who brings flowers is worth hanging on to.'

'It's only one flower mama, don't get too excited.'

'I'm not excited, I'm honoured. Thank you very much, Stelios. It is beautiful.'

'I cut it just now from a rosebush in my mother's garden which we planted together when I was a young boy. It's very special to me, to us, and I hoped it would give you pleasure to look at.'

'Oh, it does. How wonderful and I shall treasure it.'

'It's a flower, mama. It grows in soil and it dies. It's not worth getting emotional about.'

'Huh, some gifts shine as bright as the sun, but if it isn't a diamond she's not interested,' her mother huffed.

Stelios was a little hurt by Penelope's comments, but realised it was probably because the focus had been taken away from her, and it was her birthday after all.

'Speaking of shining as bright as the sun, look at you two beautiful ladies! I've never seen such wonderful glowing expressions and sparkly eyes. Did you enjoy your day at the spa?'

'Oh, yes, young man. We certainly did. I have never been so pampered and spoiled like I have today.'

'So you kept saying,' Penelope smiled kindly. 'She's had a wonderful day and we've been scrubbed and massaged and polished like you wouldn't believe.'

'Oh, that's good. I knew you were spending the day together anyway, so I thought a spa session would be a lovely thing to share. I'm glad you were made to feel special, because that's exactly what you are.'

'That's nice of you to say, dear.'

'I think he meant me, mama.'

'I mean both of you. I hadn't realised you looked so alike and tonight you really look like sisters,' he beamed.

'OK, you've gone too far now,' Penelope laughed. 'I'm just going to get my bag before you say anything else embarrassing.'

'I'm not kidding,' he said quietly to her mother once she had left the room. 'You really do look amazing.'

'I know,' she smiled. 'But let her have her moment. She enjoys being in the spotlight and she's expecting fireworks tonight, so I hope you can provide them,' she winked with the same flirtatious grin as her daughter.

'Ah, well...'

He was glad to be interrupted by Penelope's return and grabbed the bag she foisted in his direction.

'Time we were out of here,' she instructed as she kissed her mother on the cheek.

'Have a great time, kids.'

'We will,' Penelope assured her as they left the house.

'I'll put your overnight bag in the boot till later,' Stelios said as he opened her door and gave her space to get comfortable before he took the driver's seat.

'So, are you going to tell me where we're going tonight? And at what stage will I get my present?' she asked, as she pulled back the hem of her skirt to reveal beautifully toned and tanned thighs. 'Because you already know this is *your* present,' she giggled.

'I know it's hard, but you will have to wait,' he insisted with a knowing smile while trying to resist reaching over and stroking her soft, smooth legs.

'Oh, if I'd known it was hard, I would've suggested you came to my room to pick up my bag earlier and I could have done something about it!' She laughed heartily with a beautiful wide-open mouth, which he just wanted to dive on to drink in her happiness, but he wasn't sure he'd be able to stop. She was already halfway to seducing him and they hadn't even left her house.

'Difficult,' he said in a strangled voice, before clearing his throat. 'I know it's difficult to wait for your present, but you'll enjoy it more for the surprise.'

'Ooh, now I'm intrigued. So I'll put these away till we get to yours later,' she pouted for effect as she replaced her skirt to cover her legs.

'Did I say we were going to mine?' he asked suggestively as he started the engine and moved off.

'But you told me to bring an overnight bag.'

'Yes, but I didn't say where we were staying, did I?' he reminded her with a saucy smile which gave away part of the surprise, but increased her excitement, as he had known it would.

60

'Oh, where are we going? Oh, it must be that gorgeous place near Kefalos that has a private chef and butler who are on call for your every need! Or, the new all-inclusive on the far side of Kardamena that has bungalows in the grounds with a swim up pool and a free bar.'

'That's a little far…' Stelios gulped in shock. Not to mention expensive, he thought.

'Or it might be those renovated villas on the way to Thermal Springs with the stunning views over to Turkey which have private outdoor spaces for naked sunbathing.'

'Well, don't overthink it,' he said anxiously. 'Anyway, we won't be sunbathing at night.'

'No, but it's private. You know what I mean? We can be outside, naked, doing whatever we want,' she breathed with excitement as she allowed her hand to sneak up his leg towards the point of no return.

'OK, let's just slow down a bit here,' he said a little more forcefully than he'd intended as he removed her hand. She was so difficult to resist and, as he was currently driving along a quiet country road without a car in sight, he was finding it almost impossible not to just pull over and ravish her there and then.

'But you've obviously booked us into somewhere special and I'm getting excited thinking about all the things I can do to you when we get there,' she replied with a moan which was tempered with hope.

'Believe me, I'm looking forward to that too, but,' he interjected before she could say any more, 'we're going to enjoy a wonderful meal first in a spectacular setting, so let's not belittle that experience with thoughts of how we'll spend the rest of the night. Let's just appreciate it as it unfolds. We've got hours and hours to enjoy being together, it would be a shame to rush it.'

'Yes, of course, you're right,' she agreed, approving of his thoughtful speech. 'I just want to dive in and enjoy it right now.'

'Well, very soon you'll get a good idea of where we're going to eat so you can start to relax and the rest of the night will look after itself.'

'But you're driving, so unless you're not drinking, we must be staying at the same place,' she surmised sneakily, as they always had wine with their meals.

'Well, no. First we're going to a restaurant and I'll have a couple of glasses, but then we'll go on somewhere else and we can drink more there as I've already organised a fully stocked fridge.'

'Oh, you have been busy,' she said with admiration. 'And is that where I get my present?'

'Um...' He was a little stumped as the meal and the overnight stay was the gift and he wasn't really sure what to say.

'Wait a minute. Isn't this the road to Zia?'

'Yep. I knew I couldn't hide it for much longer.'

'Oh.'

'I know. It will be amazing. We'll get there just before sunset so we can eat as the sky changes colour and then enjoy our desserts by candle light.'

Stelios couldn't hide his pleasure when Smaragda revealed her idea for Penelope's birthday. He never would have thought of a mother/daughter pamper day but it was ideal for them both as he was busy working, then to have dinner at one of the best restaurants in the area at the top of the Dikaos mountain as they watched sunset over the neighbouring islands was the most perfect end to the day he could imagine.

'It will probably be busy,' she said with an air of

disappointment.

'Don't worry, my darling, I have reserved a table specially and we won't get disturbed.'

'Oh, they've closed the restaurant off for us?' she squeaked with surprise.

'Well, no, they can't do that, obviously. But we've got a table in a prime position so there won't be anyone walking in front of us or disturbing us nearby.'

'Oh, great, that makes all the difference...'

'I know, right? It's going to be so romantic and something you'll never forget,' he assured her.

'I think you're probably right there,' she said as she pulled out her phone to answer a previous notification she'd ignored.

'Look at that cute little church,' he instructed as he pointed through some trees to a hidden chapel.

'Yeah, lovely,' she replied with a nod, though Stelios didn't notice that she didn't actually look up from her phone.

'It's so beautiful around here, I can't believe we don't come more often.' Stelios decided that he would definitely schedule a run up around here and probably invite Smaragda as she was the one who'd explained why it was such a special place to her.

'A bit out of the way though,' Penelope replied as she tapped out her reply on the keyboard.

'Hey, aren't we having a date night tonight? No phones please Miss,' he laughed.

'Yeah, just answering a group chat of Happy Birthdays so they know I got all their cards and messages.'

'Oh, yes, I hope you don't mind that I posted your card through the door on the way to work. I knew you'd still be in bed but I didn't want you to have to wait till tonight.'

'No, it's fine. Oh, thanks,' she said in hindsight.

'Well, I know it wasn't anything special, but I'm making up for that tonight,' he smiled.

'Yeah, let's hope so.'

'I'm going to park here at the bottom and we can walk up to take in the view.'

'Can you drop me off then go and park?'

'Hmm. Not really. They're not keen on people holding up the road as there's no room for traffic. I'll drive through instead and park at the top and then we can walk back down past the shops and look at the trinkets.'

'You mean the souvenirs,' she scoffed. 'We're not tourists.'

'No. Quite.' He sensed a change in Penelope's mood but couldn't quite work out what had instigated it. Nevertheless, once they were seated in the prime spot at the amazing Oromedon restaurant he was sure they would enjoy the rest of the evening, with the final surprise still to be revealed.

JULY

Naomi was having a hard time checking in the passengers for the East Midlands flight.

'But it hasn't even taken off yet. Why couldn't we wait at the hotel until it's on its way?' the harassed mum of three moaned.

'Yeah. What's the point of being stuck at the gate for hours on end with no space and nothing to do? We would've been more comfortable back at the bar watching the sport channel,' the man in front with flaky sunburn complained.

'We have to keep everyone together and check in at the scheduled time,' Naomi tried to explain.

'But that's crazy,' he insisted. 'How can we check in for a flight that hasn't even taken off yet?'

'It's just delayed due to the air traffic controllers' strike in France. The UK passengers have all checked in and they're just waiting to confirm a departure time.'

'I'm going to dump my cases then go over to the café on the other side of the car park. No way I'm sitting in that tiny space for hour after hour with screaming kids, when I could be sitting in the sun with a beer.'

'What do you mean, screaming kids? They're just playing up because they're bored. If anyone needs a beer to cope with this, I think it's me!' the mother responded with increasing irritation.

'Let me just go and check on the situation,' Naomi offered in reply as she made a hasty getaway to where Mark was trying to keep all his paperwork in order.

'They're kicking off again,' she told him. 'Will you have a word? The sunburned bloke with the tartan suitcase is threatening to take off to the café over the road once he's dumped his bags.'

'OK. I'll have a chat with them. Obviously, he is allowed to do that, for future reference, but the delay will be more than three hours which means they will be entitled to some free refreshments and he won't get that if he's not in the designated gate.'

'Oh, he probably won't want to miss a freebie,' she nodded.

'Yep, that does help to keep the passengers together, but it doesn't work for everyone, so we need to let him know that he can't stay over there all afternoon or he'll miss all the updates.'

'Are there any updates for now?'

'No, but they are struggling to arrange a departure time, so if it drags on for another few hours we probably will have to get them back out and take them somewhere temporarily.'

'Oh, no, that doesn't sound good. That's kind of what they want us to do now, so if we make them squash in there and then have to move them anyway, they're going to be furious.'

'Yeah, I know, but we have to follow the guidelines. Until we know when the flight can actually leave, we can't put any plans in place at this end because it takes time to organise and costs a hell of a lot to provide coaches, rooms, food, etc.'

'Hmm, I guess so,' she conceded.

'Look, at the moment we've got a delay of around 5 hours so let's just hope it doesn't go much longer. If it gets worse, we'll deal with it as it happens, but I've been there before so I know the system and it will all work out in the end.'

'OK. Can you just calm them down a bit though, I think they'll listen to you more than me?'

'No worries, but you'll need to prepare yourself for a long stint today. We're gonna be stuck here for a while.'

'Oh, yes, of course,' she replied as he took off to speak to the guests.

Somehow, she hadn't realised that she would be there until the flight actually arrived goodness knows how many hours later. They had covered flight delays in the training, but it hadn't happened on her transfer until now, though there had been a few others who'd done one or two hours without reporting any problems.

At first, the thought depressed her as she hadn't brought any snacks to keep her going and she wasn't a fan of the burgers and nuggets they served at the kiosk, but then she realised why it would actually be more fun than she'd thought. Once the guests were all through in the departure lounge the reps would have to hang around in case of any changes, but they would be free to chat and enjoy some time together which would mean she would be able to talk to Russell in a normal way, without the craziness of the bar crawl or Greek night, or the alcohol which always made her forget her inhibitions and her resolution to stay away from him.

When they were both guiding the same event, they

always seemed to end up together at the end and, though she had enjoyed those moments, she would have preferred to have talked to him more instead of having her mouth filled with his tongue. Unfortunately, Russell took after Elvis with the vibe of 'a little less conversation, a little more action' and it was somehow getting to be their thing, however hard she tried to change it. He was just irresistible when he was flashing those cheeky grins and saucy comments, so when he made a move on her after a few drinks, it was impossible to break the mood for a 'get to know you' chat.

With this delay there would be the perfect opportunity to talk to him properly, without the silliness of the party atmosphere which was usually present and definitely without the personality changing effects of too much alcohol. They could get to know each other and she would get the chance to suggest he might visit one other night when they weren't working, so things might become maybe more official and regular. She would definitely prefer their intimate moments to take place in a private room and hopefully even in a bed, instead of behind the bushes, or under the storage space behind the bar, or in the hardly-used outdoor toilets, or on the deserted landing between the fishermen's boats – although at least that had been the most romantic memory, under a star-filled sky.

She looked over to see Mark laughing away with the guests who were checking in and was amazed at how simple he found it to ease those awkward situations. Obviously, that was why he was her Head Rep and she was glad she had such an organised and experienced supervisor because, however erratic her personal life currently was, she felt secure in her job and constantly supported by such a very easy going and relatable person.

The Kefalos rep came in to check any updates and Naomi asked her to stay with Mark's paperwork while she went back to the check in to take over from him. It seemed like she needed to stay out of the sun for a while anyway as she looked very red and breathless, so Naomi felt she was doing her a favour and believed she was being very thoughtful to look out for her colleague.

Mark stayed with her for a while before going back to his work area and the rest of the process was much less troublesome.

Once everyone had checked in and disappeared through Passport Control, the reps picked up sandwiches and snacks from the Everest catering facility and took them outside to enjoy away from prying eyes.

Russell was sitting over on the far side with Mark and another male rep, so Naomi was happy enough to eat with the other girls and chat about how their tans were coming along. After a while, the area started to get crowded with passengers for flights to Zurich and Frankfurt, which were apparently also delayed, so they moved back inside and Naomi took the opportunity to visit the toilet to freshen up. She wet-wiped her neck and cleavage and gave an extra spritz of perfume, then checked she didn't have anything stuck in her teeth before applying a glossy layer of lipstick. She was ready to chat to Russell and get to know the real person underneath the flamboyant veneer.

Some of the reps were sitting behind the old Swissair desk to be out of the way, while others were hiding out in the smoking alcove, leaving just a couple standing with Mark in his usual place. She didn't see Russell, but could hardly go searching for him. Anyway, there was plenty of time.

'Oh, Mark, you might want to see this,' a German rep called over to him, pointing to where the first floor waiting area overlooked the check in area.

Mark went over with a few reps to see what was going on and noticed a hand written sign being held up to the window with regard to their company.

'WE WERE SENT THROUGH TO THIS FLEAPIT AND JUST QUEUED FOR 25 MINUTES TO GET A CRAPPY BURGER AND CHIPS'

'Oh boy,' Mark sighed.

'Isn't that the sunburnt bloke who was complaining earlier?' Naomi asked.

'Yep, that's him.'

'Here comes another.'

'POWERADE JUST COST 6 EUROS!!! ITS A RIP OFF #NOTHAPPY'

'Wow, that's bad,' Naomi admitted.

'I agree,' Mark smirked. 'Everyone knows there should be an apostrophe in it's.'

'WE WANT A COMPLAINT FORM NOW'

'OK let's move away and see if he gets fed up,' Mark instructed as he ushered them out of sight.

'Should someone go up there and talk to him?' Naomi asked automatically, hoping that person wouldn't be her.

'No. Once they're at the departure gate they're the airport's responsibility. They'll issue vouchers for refreshments soon anyway, so he'll probably get even more miffed to have wasted his money. And we're only allowed to go through that way if the airport security request it and escort us at all times.'

'It doesn't look like he's going to calm down any time soon.'

'Well, we still haven't got any news about their flight so it's looking more and more like we're going to have to take them out again anyway.'

'Seriously?' she gasped. 'Oh, that's just going to be awful for them.'

'It might be at first, but once they get on the coaches and arrive at a nice hotel for a while most of them will calm down and make the best of the opportunity.'

'Will they go back to Kos Town?'

'No, Kardamena is closer so I've asked Russell to go and check with his hotels if they can accommodate some extra guests for the day.'

'Oh, right,' she nodded with instant disappointment.

'Hopefully he will get lucky with three or four so we don't overpower the guests already there.'

'That makes sense. How soon will he come back to let us know?'

'He'll stay there now because he'll have to oversee the operation from that end. He said he'd get someone to drive him down there in my car and then, when he has some news, he'll send them back to let us know what's available.'

'Ah, I see,' Naomi whispered as she moved away, checking all the reps as she passed. She couldn't quite work out who had disappeared until she came across the same group of girls she'd been chatting with over lunch. The Kefalos rep was nowhere to be seen and her blood ran cold as she forced the question out as to whether she had gone with Russell to sort out alternative arrangements.

'Yeah, good for them, eh? They can escape this madness,' one grumbled.

'Er, yes. Lucky them,' she half-heartedly agreed.

'Are you kidding?' the one who always wore far too

71

much make-up laughed. 'They'll be off having a joy ride round Kardamena with a cocktail in each hand if I know Russell.'

'Or checking out those hotels in detail…' another said.

'Yeah, they'll have to check out the bedrooms in case they're needed later.'

'And the bedsprings are going to be getting some workout.'

They all fell around laughing and joking about what Russell and the Kefalos rep might be getting up to while Naomi was rooted to the spot unable to move, or breathe. Finally, she was able to speak and ask the question she really didn't want to hear the answer to.

'So, are they… together, then?'

'Right now? Probably, yeah,' the make-up girl nodded, though the laughs were fading now.

'Unless she's got more sense than to fall for his chat,' her team-mate suggested.

'Like you did last year?' came the sarcastic reply.

'Well, he turned on the charm, didn't he? How was I supposed to know he did it with everyone? It hasn't worked this year though,' she confirmed with a determined scowl.

'What about you,' she nodded to Naomi. 'Any more late-night assignations since the welcome dinner?'

'Oh, what? No way,' she tutted in defence, hoping that they wouldn't notice how her legs were shaking and her teeth were chattering, regardless of the 34-degree heat.

'Yeah, he does like to dip in and dip out if you get what I mean. You're best off just having a one-off fling like most of us and don't get dragged into anything there. He's just not reliable.'

'Except you can rely on him to give us some entertainment through the summer.' And the jokes started up again as Naomi made her excuses and left them to it.

She had thought that hooking up together several times meant they were into something. Admittedly, they hadn't discussed a relationship - hadn't discussed anything really as they'd been too busy making out - but she had presumed it had been the start of something. She certainly wasn't seeing anyone else and she'd grown to think he probably wasn't either. Now she had to consider what had actually happened against what she had just heard. She knew she wouldn't be missed for a while so she sauntered down to the arrivals area to think in peace.

She relived the moments they had been alone and enjoyed remembering the excitement in the build-up to it, strengthening her resolve that they had undeniable chemistry and it was something that was always bound to happen.

She recalled what the girls had just been saying and chose to think that they would have joked the same way if it had been any other boy and girl who had escaped the grimness of an unending delay. She knew Russell was more flirtatious than most and had kissed quite a few reps (that part made her squirm with jealousy) but he obviously wasn't a bad person or an out-and-out user or they would have been slagging him off rather than just teasing.

However, she couldn't shake the feeling that when Mark had told her about Russell going back to Kardamena, he had said something along the lines of him choosing who he took with him and that was eating away at her. Did he just say it casually and she misheard it? Did Mark send them both or did Russell actually suggest it? She had been in the toilet when the decision was made, but would he have taken her instead if she'd been there?

She was feeling more and more unsettled, but with every thought she was holding on tighter to the fact that she believed they had something good together and she wasn't going to let it go without a fight. As soon as the Kefalos rep came back, she was going to ask her outright what had happened while they had been in Kardamena together, even though she couldn't get her head around the fact that they would have been getting physical while they were supposed to be working to find a solution on an urgent matter. They couldn't have done; they just simply couldn't have done.

Could they?

'Hey, Naomi,' Mark called as he approached. 'You OK?'

'Oh, I'm sorry Mark, it all just got a bit too much for me for a minute. I just needed a bit of space.'

'It's fine, everyone's been struggling a bit, but we've got some news finally.'

'Oh, great,' she smiled bravely.

'Not really. There is going to be a longer delay so we're going to transfer everyone down to Kardamena after all.'

'So it'll be a long night,' she surmised with a dreary expression, before realising what that actually meant and beaming in response. 'In Kardamena!'

'Not for you, luckily. I'm drafting in the transfer reps that were due to be on tonight's flights so that you can all go home to rest, then do their shift later instead. That way we still have cover but no one gets overly tired.'

'Oh, I see. That's very thoughtful,' she replied with less gratitude than she needed to express.

'I thought you'd be happy; the others are singing and dancing in there.'

'Yes, of course I am. That's really great. Is everyone back on tonight again then?'

'Mostly. Obviously, Russell and a couple of reps will stay in Kardamena to supervise the guests, but the rest of you will be divided up over the three smaller arrivals tonight. I'll be emailing the details through to you all once Elias sends me the paperwork later.'

'Right.'

'Pantelis is coming up from Kos Town with the transfer reps in a minibus, then he'll drive the north-side reps back to resort so will you look out for him and let the others know when he arrives?

'Yeah, no problem.'

'Thanks Naomi, you're the best,' he assured her and returned to continue with his arrangements.

'If only everyone thought so,' she murmured to herself as she realised she wouldn't get the answers she was looking for any time soon.

'Do you need a top-up?' Smaragda asked as she entered the canteen and saw Stelios gripping his mug with whitened knuckles while gazing off into space.

'Huh? Oh, no thanks.' He pushed the mug away while she made herself a drink, but soon picked it up again as though he needed to hold onto something.

'Anything wrong?'

'No. Yes. Well, no not really, but then again...'

'Oh, for heaven's sake, what's the matter?' She was concerned for Stelios' happiness, but she could she he was facing more of an inner struggle than a serious urgent issue.

'I've got myself in a bit of a bind.' He paused and Smaragda left the space open for him as he clearly needed to fill it. 'It's Penelope.'

'Mmm.' Who else could it be? He was never normally this on edge and the only thing which brought on that effect these days was Penelope. She'd noticed how he called her 'Penny' when he was loved up and feeling sentimental, but used her full name when he was boasting about her or if there was some kind of problem.

'I'm not quite sure how to deal with what happened, you know, on her birthday...'

'OK, well maybe you should try talking to *her*.' *Because I don't want to know the details.*

'I will, but I need to talk to you first. You'll understand and work out how I make her see what I really meant and how she's made a huge mistake.'

'What? Has she broken up with you?' That would, of course, be a huge mistake and not one she could imagine any sane person making.

'I'm getting this all wrong. I should start at the beginning.'

'Well, I don't have much time with all these delays going on and I'm needed on the desks, so it's probably best to get to the point,' she insisted, absolutely not in the right frame of mind to hear a blow by blow account of their romantic tryst, especially if it all ended in tears and she was expected to offer false sympathy.

'Oh, right. Well, maybe we could meet for lunch tomorrow instead and I can explain it in more detail? I don't know what to do about it and I could really use some advice from a good friend.'

Maybe it was the way he was looking at her through his long, dark lashes with those puppy dog eyes, but she couldn't really resist that plea.

'Fine, but just give me a general outline now so that I can have a think about it before tomorrow.'

'OK,' he sighed and moved in a little closer so they couldn't be overheard. 'We arrived at Oromedon for dinner and sat at the table you reserved, overlooking the coastline and out to Kalymnos.'

'It's the best table in the house,' she confirmed, imagining herself sitting there with someone to share the moment. Maybe one day.

'Well, somehow she'd become a bit edgy on the way there and then she nearly broke her neck on the cobbles through Zia's main street as she'd worn the highest heels possible and was sliding all over the place. I practically had to carry her there.'

Smaragda stifled a giggle as she had never had that problem with the stylish, but sensible, shoes she normally wore.

'Yes, I see you smiling, but she was not impressed and she got so annoyed that even the fantastic view from the restaurant couldn't undo her irritation.'

'That's a shame,' Smaragda said with as much

sympathy as she could muster. She had organised what she considered the most perfect date possible and the fact that Penelope had been too selfish to recognise that was frustrating. Though she couldn't understand how it would get so much worse that she would have finished with him.

'We had a really delicious meal and the service was excellent, but she spent most of the time on her phone replying to birthday messages and wasn't impressed by the fabulous sunset at all.'

'That's not possible,' Smaragda replied automatically as it was one of the most spectacular sights that Kos was famous for.

'She said she'd seen better in Santorini and Crete, but I haven't been there yet so I couldn't argue.'

'So, she was generally in a mood.' Typical diva behaviour, she thought. 'Even after the pamper session at the spa?'

'Oh no, she loved that. She was really buzzing when I picked her up and as we set off. She just seemed to wind down as we arrived in Zia. I think she was expecting a bit more.'

'More what?' How could anyone expect more than a romantic dinner in Zia? It was perfect.

'She seemed to think we should be going to a private villa with our own chef, or booked into an all-inclusive for the night. She was expecting five-star luxury.'

'But you were hardly slumming it. And why on earth would anyone want to stay overnight in an all-inclusive?'

'I know, but she was hoping for the kind of treat she's dreamed of, rather than just something a little bit better than usual.'

'So it all went downhill from there.' Smaragda really

didn't want to hear any more about how Penelope disliked the things she considered a dream and she didn't want to waste her time listening to her views on anything else.

'Well, she did relax a bit after a bottle of wine and a couple of shots. By the end of the meal we were laughing and sharing a very naughty dessert.'

'Well that sounds… better?'

'She knew we were going on to somewhere else so we decided to move while the mood was still light. I brought the car round to pick her up so she didn't have to stagger back over the cobbles, even though I got shouted at by a few of the business owners for blocking the street when she took forever to say goodnight to the staff.'

'You can't park up in the street; I thought you knew that,' she reprimanded him.

'Yes, but you also can't argue with a beautiful woman,' he shrugged.

Ouch.

'So you turned up at the traditional house in Asfendiou?'

'Yeah. It didn't make a great impression.'

'It's beautiful,' she gulped in disbelief.

'You'd think so, but she was expecting five-star shiny glitz, with all mod cons.'

'It's traditional. The clue is in the description.'

'I know, but she wanted cable TV and a sauna and fairy lights in the bedroom.'

'Oh God, seriously?' Smaragda could not believe the cheek of the woman.

'Yeah. To be honest, it didn't look great in the dark. A lot of its appeal is in the whitewashed walls and the spectacular view, but none of it was obvious in the dark.

Plus, the cockerel was going hell for leather which didn't help.'

'But it's so private and romantic.'

'You'd think so, but she just saw an old shack. She'd expected a secluded garden and at least a pool.'

'There's a hot tub!' she pointed out, remembering how she'd imagined relaxing in it with someone special and watching the stars as they shared a romantic moment.

'Yeah, in the end that was what saved the day.'

'Oh?' *Please don't spoil my vision.*

'Well that's where it got better and worse all at the same time.'

'Look, I'm running out of time,' Smaragda said as she tried to avoid listening to what they had got up to in the hot tub. 'Tell me the rest tomorrow.' She moved her chair to prepare to stand.

'That's almost it,' he assured her by placing his hand on her arm. 'Let me finish, please.'

She couldn't understand the feeling she experienced as the perfect romantic image in the hot tub combined with the warm but gentle touch of his skin on hers. It was very unsettling and weird.

'OK, but I need the short version.' *No intimate details please.*

'Well I showed her the hot tub and she seemed a bit happier so I cracked open the champagne and we drank the first glass quickly, taking the rest outside. The cockerel was making a din and she wasn't happy about it, saying there were too many disturbances and she couldn't feel relaxed.'

'Hmm.' There was plenty to say in reply, but it wasn't the right time. She would wait until tomorrow and then give him all the reasons he was better off without her.

'I assured her that there was no one else around except us and we had all the privacy we needed as, and I think I'm remembering this right, I told her "It's all ours" meaning we wouldn't be disturbed.'

'Right.' That sounded so perfectly romantic, she just couldn't imagine how anyone would break up with him after that.

'Next minute she's ripping my clothes off and pulling me into the tub for the wildest night I've ever had. Honestly, she's never been that excited, happy or willing to please me in all the time we've been together.' His eyes were bright, although that contrasted strangely with the perplexed look he was also exhibiting.

Smaragda couldn't speak as her throat had constricted to such a point that she was finding it hard to breathe.

'We were up most of the night and in the moments when we were just taking a few minutes to catch our breath, she was saying how a little light here and an extra cupboard there would make all the difference. I really thought she was starting to see the beauty in the place.'

She really should say something but she just wanted him to get it over with and stop talking so that she didn't have to imagine what had happened in the place she'd hoped would hold all her romantic memories. She simply nodded for him to continue.

'In the morning I found out why she'd been imagining how to improve the place and this is the problem I don't know how to solve.'

Smaragda shrugged, though she was getting the feeling things were not panning out as she had expected.

'When I told her the place was all ours, I meant for the night, without disturbances. She thinks I've bought the place for us to share. I have no idea what to do.'

They stared at each other for several seconds. Stelios was drained and Smaragda was stunned. It took a few breaths to gather her thoughts.

'But you told her she was mistaken, and that's when she broke up with you?'

'No, and... No. We haven't broken up, why would you say that?'

'That's what you said at the beginning, I think?' She doubted herself now but she thought that was what the whole conversation had been about.

'I didn't, because we haven't. After the birthday celebration we're stronger than ever. The only problem is she thinks I've bought her this fantastic gift.'

'Just tell her she made a mistake. It's not something you can fake. The longer you leave it the worse it'll be and then she'll definitely break up with you.'

'That's why I need to know how to tell her. I can't just come straight out with it. Maybe I can say the seller backed out?'

'And then you'll have to buy a replacement present which won't come anywhere near as close. Didn't you explain that the spa session, dinner and the traditional house were the gifts? That should be more than enough for anyone.'

'She just got it into her head and she was so happy I couldn't tell her it wasn't true. We were just having such a good time and things were finally back on track again once we hit the hot tub, I really didn't want to spoil it.'

'And now, here you are.'

'Here I am. Help me please, sister. I know you can make this better.'

That was it, she couldn't take any more of this.

'OK, I'll have a think and meet you for lunch tomorrow at the usual place.'

'Bus station?'

'Yes, where else?' It was the café they always used for private chats they didn't want friends or family to overhear as its main customers were generally the bus drivers and passengers.

'You're a lifesaver; you know that, don't you?' he announced openly as they made their way back to work.

She smiled and nodded her response but inside she wondered how she always ended up saving other peoples' lives, when her own was floundering so badly.

Penelope was organising the storage of the duty-free goods bought by the delayed passengers who were temporarily leaving the airport, as they had to be kept safely locked up until the flight was ready to board.

Some of the passengers were arguing that they had bought the items and were justified in taking them away, although the rep who had been allowed airside was doing a good job of putting them straight.

He was having a difficult time with one man who had spent too long in the sun as far as Penelope was concerned, because he wanted to take his vodka with him to drink later as it was cheaper than buying a few glasses in a hotel. The rep called the airport security over and they held their guns as they explained the procedure and he finally handed over his bag.

It was a little bit annoying as she had to label everything and push the trolley around to the storage unit on her own while her two colleagues were being kept busy by the German and Swiss passengers who were still waiting for their flight and constantly popping in and out of the duty-free shop for snacks and toys for their kids.

At least when she got there and took her time unloading the goods, she had a chance to think about everything that had happened on her birthday.

The daytime pamper session had been absolutely wonderful. She'd thoroughly enjoyed spending time with her mum and getting all the lovely treatments which made her feel even more attractive than usual. She was feeling quite sexy and looking forward to a night out with Stelios and trying to imagine what amazing gift he was going to buy for her.

As she was getting ready at home, she had received a notification on Facebook and was speechless to see it was a short message from the Shakira lookalike. She said she'd been thinking of her and had been happy to find her on Facebook, then ecstatic to discover it was actually her birthday. She sent lots of hugs and kisses and hoped she had a fantastic day.

Her finger had hovered to reply instantly, but then she stopped as her heart thundered violently under her blouse.

Firstly, what to say? The message she had received had been brief, but full of feeling without any excess emotion. She couldn't guarantee that she could hit the same mood and didn't want to come off too detached, or go to the opposite extreme and appear too invested.

Secondly, she could end up in a long conversation if her return message was desired and well received. She hadn't asked how Penelope was doing, or where she was going for her birthday so she probably wasn't waiting for an answer, but if she replied immediately it would be obvious that she wanted to be in touch and they might end up nattering forever like they so easily used to do.

Thirdly, and here was the problem, Stelios. Her response to Shakira's message (she always called her Shakira in her head to avoid ever saying her given name out loud in the real world) had been so immediate and unflinching, she was scared what that reaction meant. Obviously, any reminder of those unbelievably perfect lazy days in her company always put a smile on her face and a tingle in her nether regions, but it was in the past and she had moved on. She loved Stelios. He was her future and things were going really well for them. She'd even trusted him enough to tell him the one thing that turned her on, without fail, every single time it was done and she was so completely ecstatic with the way their love-making continued to improve that she was not about to jeopardise it by getting distracted with an emotional connection on Facebook. Even if it was with the exact person who had introduced her to that impeccable sexual sensation in the first place.

So she had decided to postpone her reply till the next day when she could fill the message with all the ways she had enjoyed her day and aim for a friends-only vibe.

As she put the finishing touches to her outfit, she realised that she had retained the sexy mood she had experienced earlier and it had, in fact, been enhanced by the out-of-the-blue message just then. She really wished she could just go and meet Stelios at his house so they could fall into bed straight away and take advantage of this extreme feeling while it was so strong, but hopefully he wouldn't be able to resist her for too long and they might make a quick detour before they went out.

Then she relived the disappointment as he couldn't be tempted to touch her and allow her to release the passion that had built inside her. To then find they were going up to the shabby mountain villages for something traditional (let's call it basic, she thought) to eat, then stay over in what looked like a badly converted barn, was more disappointing than she could have imagined. He'd let her think they would be waited on hand and foot by willing staff in an expensive and executive villa with all the mod cons, only to end up sitting outside (outside!) on a draughty mountain top, then slumming it in some old person's house with very little electricity and no wi-fi.

The only break in the monotony came when she decided to reply to Shakira's message with the news that she was happy to hear from her and was currently being whisked away to goodness knew where for an evening of treats and surprises.

Of course, she had replied immediately and a short back and forth had begun, giving her that much needed boost of flattery that she needed to get through what was becoming a very dissatisfying birthday. There were hints of flirtation without any obvious declarations, but she knew she shouldn't be having that kind of conversation while she was on a date with her boyfriend and that made it all the more spicy.

She had decided to relax and down a few drinks to make the bad feeling disappear and nipped to the toilet a few times to have a taste of the vodka she had popped in her bag for extra zip, in addition to the drinks Stelios thought he was treating her to.

By the time they were leaving the restaurant, she had wrapped up the messaging with a promise to give an update the next day and was determined to forget the disappointments and concentrate on having a good night with Stelios. That was shattered when they simply drove to the next village and she stepped into her worst nightmare.

She had been about to drink herself into a stupor when Stelios revealed that the place was now theirs and she was so surprised by the extent of his generosity and obvious love for her that she jumped on him and didn't let him go until her passion had been properly and repeatedly extinguished.

The place was a wreck, but the fact that he had bought them a secret love nest was so obviously a declaration of commitment, she was able to overlook the gloomy interiors and imagine all the changes they could make to create a bright, modern and luxurious private space for them to enjoy forever. It wouldn't be their proper home (as if!) but it could be made good enough for overnight getaways where they could frolic naked under the stars.

She'd had a momentary wobble over her relationship with Stelios when he had got her birthday location so wrong, but he had made up for it with the bare bones of his surprise gift which was easily repairable and a lasting token of his love.

She was now sure she could have a happy future with him, even though images of Shakira had invaded her thoughts while they had been getting intimate in the hot tub, then the bed, then the kitchen sink, then the hot tub again, and finally the bed again, and again, and again.

It was the first time she had come to mind when she was making love with Stelios and it had definitely made things more intense and physical, but she had to separate the two and concentrate on her future with him.

She told herself the same thing over and over but couldn't somehow bear to let Shakira go. She would have to be strong, as they were obviously never going to meet again, but finding a way to be Facebook friends might be enough if she could avoid the temptation to chat when she was feeling particularly needy or overlooked.

Hopefully Stelios would ramp up his attention now they had entered a new phase and show her how wonderful their future together was going to be. She was looking forward to lots more of his lovely treats and surprises.

AUGUST

'Can we stop here for a bit?' Smaragda panted as she brought her bicycle to a halt under the shade of a large eucalyptus tree, with a very convenient bench underneath.

'Can't take the pace, eh?' Stelios laughed as he drew up alongside with hardly a hair out of place.

'Well, that hill was a bit steeper than I'd expected and it's only my second time on this thing.'

'I know, I'm only teasing. You're actually doing really well since you're not used to cycling. Better than I thought, actually,' he added with respect.

'I feel like death,' she laughed as she collapsed on the bench and drank heartily from her water bottle.

'You are a bit pink, so this is probably as good a spot as any to have a rest.'

'It's lovely, isn't it?' She paused to look around. 'I've enjoyed visiting Pyli village before, but it was always in a car, so to be able to smell the flowers and hear the birds and touch the grasses as we cycle through is a wonderful new experience.'

'Even when you're cursing me at the same time for putting you out of your comfort zone?'

'Well, I'm used to how my body feels when I'm running, but this is completely different. My legs are literally on fire!'

'Not now,' Stelios laughed as he tipped some of his water over them.

'Oh, thanks,' she nodded with fake sarcasm. In actual fact, it was quite cooling on her bare legs and she was glad she'd worn her shorts instead of leggings.

'My pleasure,' he bowed. 'It's nice to have the company and it'll work different parts of your body than just running.'

'Yeah, if I don't collapse first,' she replied as she swept her hands across her legs to feel the cooling effect of the water all over.

'Hey, you've got a good tan. When did that happen?' he asked in surprise as he noticed that her legs were also looking more toned and healthy.

'I've been going to that little bay you told me about, where you like to swim?' she reminded him. 'It really is as peaceful and calm as you said, so I've enjoyed a few morning dips there and then made the most of drying off in the sun.'

'Nice. It suits you,' he said with genuine surprise, as he was astonished that his regular running buddy suddenly looked like a very attractive woman and his body was reacting in the usual way.

'So, what's going on with you?' she asked, to deflect the weird feeling that had started in her stomach as he'd complimented her out of the blue with a strange twinkle in his eyes.

'Nothing! What do you mean?' he asked guiltily. *He didn't even understand what had just happened with* that physical sensation, so how on earth did *she* know?

'I mean, what's happening in your life? Have you broken the news to Penelope about the house yet?' Why did she have to bring up Penelope now? That was about the worst subject she could have introduced during some kind of special moment between them.

'Oh, that,' he replied sullenly, as the mention of his girlfriend's name poured cold water on whatever had just crossed his mind moments earlier. He wasn't sure if the sudden slump in his mood was due to guilt, or the reminder of the unpleasant scenario he was currently managing with Penelope herself.

'Yes, that. Please tell me you've come clean and told her about the mistake.'

'I tried.'

'There is no try, there is only do,' she said robotically, to paraphrase a well-known Yoda quote.

'Well, I did get into the conversation that I hadn't actually bought the house,' he hesitated. 'But she didn't quite understand.'

'What's not to understand? You didn't buy the house. End of.'

'Well, she took that to mean I haven't bought it, yet.'

'I don't think I want to hear this,' Smaragda thought to herself before realising she had actually said it out loud.

'Well, it's not my fault. She's so hung up on having this little getaway place where we can escape to for the night… It's very hard to disappoint her.'

'I'm sure you could never disappoint her,' she responded, again having meant to only think the words.

'Well, this is it. I don't want to let her down now, when it seems I've finally done something right. I don't want to blow it if I can find a way around it.'

'What do you mean by 'finally' done something right? I thought things had been going right from the beginning? And, can I remind you, there's no way around it as you haven't bought the house and won't be buying it in the future!'

'I know that and you know that, but she doesn't.'

'But she's going to find out soon, so why don't you just get it over with.'

'It's not that easy.'

'Yes, it is. You just say "I didn't buy it" and apologise for giving her the wrong idea.'

'But she thought I'd done this amazing thing for her and she was so happy.'

'Well, she won't be happy when she finds out you've been lying. And you can't be happy when you have to lie to your girlfriend to keep her in the dark,' she snapped. She couldn't believe Stelios was capable of such duplicity, especially with someone he was supposed to care for. She wouldn't be able to live with it if he ever treated her that way.

'You don't get it...' he replied with a shrug as he hung his head and sighed pitifully.

Smaragda's heart jumped at the sight of her friend in such confusion. She couldn't agree with what he was doing, but she could see he was struggling to own up and, although she didn't know the reason why he was so torn, she realised she had to support his decision and be there to mop up the pieces if it all blew up in his face.

'Why don't you try me?' she asked gently. 'If pretending to buy a house is that important to you, help me to understand why you think that's the only thing that you think you have 'finally' done right, to quote your earlier comment.'

'I dunno. Shall we cycle on to the next village? I might get things straight in my head with a bit more exercise.'

Smaragda hesitated to reply as she didn't want to force Stelios into an awkward conversation, but felt the mood was right for the opportunity to open up and say what was really on his mind.

'I don't think I'm ready just yet, can we sit here a little longer until I get over these muscle cramps in my legs?'

'Oh, yeah, of course. I didn't realise you were struggling with that. Shall I massage them? Or you can,' he added quickly as they both did a double take at his unexpectedly personal suggestion.

'No, they're not too bad. If I can just rest a little longer, I'll be fine.'

'Good.'

She worried that the tone of the conversation had become stilted, but had to try to bring it back to what was troubling him. She waited a moment, took a breath and went into best friend mode as she began slowly.

'What do you think would happen if Penelope understood that she'd made a mistake and you hadn't actually bought the house but just rented it for the night?'

'She'd be furious.'

'Because you lied to her.'

'No, because she was having an awful birthday up to that point and it was the only thing that saved the night.'

Smaragda once again raged inside at the fact that she had given up her idea for the most perfect evening she could imagine and someone else had reacted as though it was a punishment.

'But then she saw the beauty in being there, at that point, at least,' she offered optimistically.

'I thought so initially, but then I realised she was just imagining how she could improve it to match her needs and expectations.'

'Well, we all like different accessories,' she replied diplomatically. 'I guess she could see how a few little extras would make things nicer for her.' She was being polite but could not understand for a moment why anyone would want to change the tiniest detail of that immaculately cosy and traditional hideaway.

'Forget 'little extras' and replace it with a complete renovation. She was remodelling the whole place by the time we left.'

'So she wouldn't have enjoyed it as a one-night treat in a traditional setting?'

'Not a chance. Things were going downhill fast until she believed I had actually bought it. Then the dollar signs started flashing and she presumably thought it gave her some kind of status to own a property even if it was, as she put it, in the sticks.'

'But that would be one hell of a present. Surely she couldn't really think you'd bought it? For her?'

'She really did. The way she reacted was like nothing I've ever seen before. The thing is, we always have a good time together, if you know what I mean, but,' he continued quickly as he had to get it off his chest, 'that night was totally different. Totally. She was insatiable and getting a real kick out of what she thought was her birthday gift. Her face was alight with pleasure and happiness and I couldn't get enough of it.'

'I can imagine,' Smaragda responded with fake understanding as her body was doing the most unpleasant things while trying to ignore the thought of

Stelios writhing naked with the perfect Penelope and was refusing to release the image of his ecstatic face in the throes of passion. She wasn't used to thinking of her close friend that way, but it was becoming a habit recently and that was just weird.

'No, I don't mean like that. Well, I probably do, but also it was the first time I'd felt that the reason she was enjoying herself so much was because of *me*. *I* was the one who had given her that new found sense of position, of superiority. Usually she's the one with all the power and I just feel like I'm doing my duty, but this time it was all happening because of me and I felt like I was actually... worth something,' he ended breathlessly.

Smaragda was also breathless. She was still fighting the images, but then to hear Stelios saying he hadn't been feeling worthy was impossible to accept.

'I don't think I understand,' she gasped.

'Let me rephrase that,' he said gently as he took a few breaths to calm his racing heart. 'When I first got together with Penelope, I couldn't believe my luck, you know? She's so beautiful I thought she was kidding when she agreed to go out with me, but we hit it off straight away and we seemed to have so much in common.'

'Oh?' Smaragda queried, as she couldn't imagine that being the case.

'Well, we seemed to chat on and on and soon we were spending the night together and it was really amazing. She introduced me to some unique moves and we were really in tune for a while.'

'A while?' She'd thought they had been 'in tune' all the time.

'Yeah, we were really having fun, but recently it seems to have become a bit of an effort to keep her interested. We enjoy our meals out, but she wants to try something new all the time. We've done Chinese, Indian, Thai, Korean, Spanish, Australian, Moroccan, Turkish and even Danish, but she still wants something different.'

'Wow! That's some list.'

'And we still have fun in the bedroom,' he said convincingly, 'but we've got used to doing all the things she likes and if I try something else she doesn't want to know. She's still perfectly satisfied, so she doesn't think there's anything wrong, but it's all feeling a bit mechanical now. It's been on her terms since the beginning and I haven't felt like an equal until her birthday, but that night I was the one who had instigated that reaction and it felt amazing.'

'Well, that must have been nice.' Smaragda could not believe that Stelios would ever feel less than amazing as he was the most worthwhile human being she knew, but she could see it was his honest view of the relationship. She was glad he'd experienced a moment where he felt at least equal to his girlfriend, but she wished he knew how far above that he really was.

'She's a beautiful woman and she felt special that night, because of me. How can I admit it was all a mistake and I'm not the person she thought I was?'

'So what will you do? You can't actually buy the place. I don't think it would even be for sale.'

'I've said that the owner lives in Athens and isn't coming over until the end of the season so I'll have to wait till then to sort all the paperwork. As we're both working, we wouldn't be able to do any renovations till winter anyway so she's a bit miffed, but agreed to wait for now.'

'That gives you some breathing space, but you'll have to own up eventually.'

'I know and it's on my mind all the time,' he admitted. 'But with you to distract me,' he turned and gave her a grateful smile, 'I can think about other things. Happier things.'

'Like what?' she asked in surprise, glad of his shift to an upbeat mood.

'Like the big works do for the Dekapentavgoustos celebration on the 15th next week. But mostly, how I'm going to beat you to the next village,' he challenged as he stood and prepared to mount his bike again.

'OK,' she laughed, 'but the first one there buys the baklava.'

'Shouldn't that be the last one there?' he called over his shoulder as he set off.

'No, the last one there gets to eat it!' she called triumphantly.

Mark let Russell know he was the first to arrive at the airport and needed to take his guests through to check-in desks 4 and 5 for the Manchester flight.

'Can I stay inside with them today and man the desks and luggage scanner?'

'If you want to. I thought you preferred being outside with the guests, keeping them entertained,' Mark asked with a smirk as he repeated Russell's favourite phrase.

'Yeah, that's great, but I haven't done this bit for ages so it'd be nice for a change.'

'Doesn't worry me. Does that mean you don't have any besotted guests to keep company before they leave today?'

'All my guests are besotted. I thought you knew that.'

'Obviously. No one that you especially want to spend time with? Or are you trying to avoid someone?'

'Well, they'll all be in here with me, won't they?' he replied in conclusion. 'I'd better go and bring them in.'

Mark left him to it and only realised as he re-entered the building that the wonderful air conditioning made a massive difference on a hot August day. Clearly, Russell had thought ahead.

The check-in desk was already open and the other reps soon arrived, so he let them organise the departures while he updated the arrivals list which had a couple of alterations.

He was just about finishing up when he got a call from Jane in the office to say they had just been notified of another twelve passengers who had booked the holiday type they all feared – allocation on arrival.

It meant there were flight seats to sell at the last moment, but there was not necessarily any information about available accommodation and the passengers had to agree to be placed wherever there was a room free once they got to the arrivals hall.

It was something most of the travel companies used and usually there were a few free rooms in their guaranteed properties, or cheap rooms for rent in the more basic hotels they had relationships with, but occasionally they were all booked up and the staff had to quickly find new accommodation which was clean and ready with, hopefully, all the correct health and safety certificates in place.

The problem with that procedure was it usually happened in peak season when all the other accommodation had already been booked up for months. It was also a race against time because they were only advised of changes as the flight departed the UK. The poor holidaymakers had no idea of the system used for their holiday when they booked an hour before departure; they presumed the seats were available so the rooms must also be available, they just wouldn't know which one they were going to get until they arrived. They also believed that if they didn't like the sound of the resort, they could refuse and simply say they would just take one of the rooms in the resort they preferred instead.

Mark regularly thought the company should make clear to the customer exactly what the process entailed at the point of purchase, because the resort reps were always the ones who took the flak and had to deflect all the abuse and complaints that inevitably resulted from the dissatisfying room or location. They weren't allowed to explain the complicated procedure of ringing around every hotel they knew to secure a room for them to use as it came across as unprofessional and haphazard.

That's exactly what it was, but they weren't allowed to know that because it spoiled the company's reputation and also gave them good grounds for a complaint. Imagine admitting that they had accepted money for a holiday when they didn't even have a room for that person to stay?

That was the problem Mark was now facing as twelve unexpected arrivals had been added to the flight manifest with no rooms waiting for them. The girls in the office were ringing around their emergency list of possible alternatives of places they knew had acceptable health and safety procedures, while they asked Mark to ring around some of his local friends to see if they knew of any independent units that were rented by the day to casual visitors, who usually arrived on the ferries.

He was just in the middle of his third call to ask for assistance and hoping they weren't fully booked like the previous two, when the Kefalos rep appeared before him with a face like thunder. He held up his hand as he listened to the person on the other end.

'Just a second,' he whispered as he started writing down some information.

'So you've got one room tonight, but only for 5 days? OK. Then you have two more rooms from Thursday for 9 days? And how much per night? Hmm. And that's room only or self-catering? I see. Well, thank you. I'll call back if it fits in with what we need.'

He sighed and replaced his pen with a show of calmness he definitely didn't feel.

'OK, how's it going out there?' he asked reluctantly.

'Can you please tell Naomi to stop referring me to her guests as a southerner? There's one bloke who's had too much to drink and he won't let it drop. She thinks it's funny.'

'Wait, what? You're not a southerner. Aren't you from Bristol or something?'

'Bath. But she doesn't mean that. She means Kefalos. Apparently, anything upwards from the airport and Kardamena is classed as the north side so down in the depths of Kefalos I'm apparently a southerner which is wrong on so many levels.'

'OK, well I'm just busy with an emergency at the moment, so I'll have a word with her later, but just ignore the guest; he'll be checking in for his flight soon enough and you won't have to hear any more about it.'

'Huh,' she pouted and stormed off.

He continued to call the few numbers he'd been given by his friends Costas and Maria, who used to run the Aegean Sun Hotel where he'd first been made to feel like a local. He trusted them to suggest decent places, but in peak season it wasn't a guarantee any of them would be available.

Jane called and let him know they had found three rooms, so they just needed three more and he was frustrated that he didn't have anything to offer himself.

'Don't worry, Mark. We'll find something.'

'I hope so. The last place I just spoke to was in the middle of nowhere and the prices were ridiculous. With these last-minute sales being such a cheap bargain, I don't know if we'll even be able to cover the cost, never mind make a profit.'

'Well, if that's the case, maybe they'll learn not to sell off the seats willy-nilly. If the only rooms we can get are in a five-star hotel, what do they expect us to do?'

'I guess Elias hasn't told you what happens in emergencies if it comes down to the wire?' he asked cautiously.

'Noooo…?' she replied warily.

'If we haven't found anything and they end up in an expensive room for the first night, we are supposed to inform the reps staying in guaranteed units and they have to move out to make space for the extra bookings and just have to share with other reps until the end of the period.'

'You're kidding?'

'I am so not kidding. I've done it a couple of times myself but I don't mind bunking up with someone temporarily. Can't say the same for some of this year's reps though, if that's gonna happen.'

'Oh, crikey. I'd better get on and try to find something,' she said.

'Good luck with that.'

'You too, bye.'

Mark needed a drink and some fresh air, but he wasn't ready to deal with whatever was going on outside with the Kefalos rep and Naomi, so he picked up his phone and made several more calls until he finally found a place with one room. It was better than nothing.

'That's good,' Elias told him. 'I've heard of that place so I'll go there now and discuss the details with the owner. Thanks a lot for phoning around. We only need one more room and Jane's on to a possibility right now. It looks like we're going to be AOK.'

'Great. All's well that ends well,' he breathed as he put down his phone and decided to have a break.

'Mark, you need to come over to the check-in right now. We've got a problem,' Russell informed him as he immediately turned round to head back to the area in question.

Mark trailed along but could hear the kerfuffle

before he arrived.

'Seriously, whassa problem?' the man was shouting as Smaragda was asking him to step back, away from the desk. 'I got my ticket, I got my passport, I got my woman. Jus' lemme on the plane.'

'OK, we need to step back, sir, so that we can sort out what's going on here,' Mark advised.

'Nofinks goin' on. We're trynna check in but she won't take our tickets.'

'Obviously there's something wrong here,' Mark offered sympathetically in order to gain the man's confidence. 'Why don't you and your good lady take a seat at the side and I'll go and check your tickets to see what the issue is. You won't lose your place in the queue as I'll see to it myself when it's sorted.'

'Uh, OK,' he replied, glad that someone was looking after him properly.

'Which resort did you come in from, by the way?'

'Kos Town, innit?'

'Lovely. You just wait here and I'll be back as soon as I can.'

He went back to Russell and asked him to go and fetch Naomi inside.

'Oh, no can-do boss. Smaragda wants me to assist them with the luggage scanner as there's some oldies who can't lift it up,' he shrugged.

'Fine,' he growled and went out to find her himself. He gave her a dressing down for allowing a passenger to either board the coach drunk, or get drunk on the way and for not informing said passenger that if he didn't sober up, he wouldn't be allowed on the flight.

'Now you can go and get some coffees and sit with him to let him know what's going on.'

'I honestly didn't realise, I just thought he was a

loudmouth.'

'Well, there's usually a reason for that, isn't there?' He was having a bad day and it wasn't getting any better.

'I was just glad he wasn't slagging me off because he seemed to enjoy that with the other reps. And he doesn't like southerners, that's for sure,' she said.

'Wait a minute. Did you set him off on hating Kefalos because it's in the south of the island?'

'No, of course not. He asked what the name of that resort was because he never got to go there, but when I told him he started taking the mickey and saying it sounded poncey, like all southerners. He wouldn't let it rest but I couldn't get through to him.'

'And you didn't come and tell me what was happening because...'

'Because I didn't want to come inside and... erm... disturb you.'

'Oh, for goodness' sake. You don't want to come inside. Russell doesn't want to go outside. I've got one rep blaming another for slagging her off and in the midst of it all I've got twelve people arriving soon and no idea as yet which coach I need to put them on.'

'Why would Russell...?'

'I don't want to hear it!' he interrupted her. 'Just go and sober up your guest while you've still got time. Make him understand he seriously might not get on that plane if he doesn't. These are his tickets; just say I've checked them and they'll be fine once he's sobered up.'

He pushed the paperwork on her and sent her off, before he went to chill out in the smokers' alcove for ten minutes.

After a few deep breaths and a quick phone chat

with Zoe, he calmed down and realised he'd been a bit harsh with Naomi, but seriously, what was going on with her? She was usually calm and organised, but today she seemed to be all over the place. The Kefalos rep wasn't much better, jumping to conclusions without trying to sort things out properly. He would never understand women generally.

He was glad he understood Zoe and was looking forward to getting these arrivals out of the way so he could return to her side and get it all off his chest. She would make it all better and tomorrow things would be back to normal, at least for him. The reps, however, seemed to have some issues between them and he was going to stay well out of the way while they sorted it all out.

On the evening of the 15th, the airport staff were attending a party in town for the celebration of the Dormition of the Virgin Mary, the biggest event on the Greek calendar after Easter and Christmas.

Stelios had collected Penelope from her house and they were chatting to a few colleagues as they enjoyed a drink before the meal began.

Penelope had somehow brought up the subject of house renovations and people were commenting on which builders to use or avoid and what their dream house would look like. She had been asked not to tell anyone about the new purchase as Stelios didn't want people poking their noses in before it was all signed and sealed, but he had promised a large house-warming party when it had been finalised.

He knew he was taking a chance, but hoped she would go along with his request in the expectation of a bigger pay off down the line as she believed she would get full rein on her renovation plans.

Of course, she couldn't resist testing him and secretly enjoyed the thrill of knowing why she was instigating this particular conversation without letting the cat out of the bag. It was stimulating to feel she was somehow better than them and even though they didn't know it yet, they would find out very soon as she was not going to hide it for too long.

The group were droning on about conservatories and tinted glass so Stelios tuned out and wondered about his current situation. Penelope had agreed to keep the news - or the lie, as he knew it was - to themselves for the moment but it didn't stop the fact that the truth would come out at some point.

He'd decided that he would have to concoct some kind of story where the imaginary owner had changed their mind and didn't want to sell, but he knew Penelope would want to get on the phone to convince them herself and obviously that wouldn't be feasible.

Another possibility was that the owner was ill and had to stay in Athens indefinitely, but that wasn't a final solution as she would still want some contact details to get involved herself if she had begun negotiations for the renovations.

He could go for broke and say the owner had died and the property was being left to the family, who didn't want to sell. That seemed like the unquestionable resolution, until he realised that once she had accepted the fact, she would simply look for another property instead as he would owe her the gift he had originally promised.

He couldn't see a way of getting out of the problem unless he actually told her the truth that he had never intended to buy a house and, more to the point, wasn't able to afford to do so. He knew without a doubt that she would dump him faster than the speed of light and he wasn't sure how he'd cope with that.

That thought alone was a puzzle because he should have thought that he wouldn't be able to cope without her whatsoever, that he would be devastated and want to hang on to her if at all possible, but it was true that he just didn't know how he'd react.

When he'd realised that he had (supposedly) acted in a style which had made Penelope see him in a different way, in a much better way, he had been ecstatic at the thought of being good enough for her and he was proud and happy to be an equal with her. However, in the days since, he had recognised that he'd seen himself as much less than worthwhile up until that point, even though he had been feeling lucky to be having such an intimate and physical relationship with such a goddess.

Those lucky feelings and, he had to admit, the sexual encounters, were such a boost to his ego he had initially ignored some of the frustrating habits she had and the way they always did the things *she* wanted to do. He'd put up with some derogatory comments and light-hearted put downs as a way of challenging himself to do better as a boyfriend and as a man.

He'd pretended not to notice the times when she threw up after a meal as she was always so proud of her flat stomach and he hadn't complained when she pressed his mouth against it.

He'd gone along with the way she orchestrated where they would go, who they would see, what he would wear and how fast or slow their bedroom sessions would be.

He thought he'd finally broken the spell when she believed he'd bought the traditional stone house and hoped things would change for the better, but after a week that bubble had burst and all she'd been interested in was all the new things she could buy to update the property and how she'd need a professional interior designer to get it right.

She obviously now expected him to provide the funds to make the house suitable to her own extravagant tastes, regardless of the fact that he didn't even have enough to buy it in the first place.

That initial explosion of desire she'd had for him, which had come from her mistaken belief that he could provide expensive gifts, had quickly faded into an assumption that she could now expect that on a regular basis.

Their love-making had once again become

perfunctory. They were both satisfied physically as they were both experienced enough to achieve that result, but he no longer felt like he was properly connecting on an emotional level and he was aware that he could not continue to imagine he was still her equal, as he had temporarily believed himself to be.

He felt like a kid at the sweet shop who spends all his birthday cash on the beloved chocolate delights he has dreamed about for the last year. He's out of his mind with happiness to be enjoying something he thought he would never get and takes as much as he can while he has the opportunity then, as he relishes his conquest and appreciates the achievement of an impossible fantasy, he realises that what remains doesn't have the same exquisite quality and he's just continuing with the rest because it's available and he can't turn away.

Apart from the sex, which he could never refuse as that was his form of chocolate treat, they really didn't have that much in common and he didn't feel that she respected his choices or views.

He enjoyed the times they went out for dinner and tried lots of new cuisine and foreign wines, but she wasn't really relishing that fact if she just brought it all back some time later to avoid the weight gain. He'd tried to persuade her to join him for a regular swim, hoping that she'd enjoy it enough to allow that exercise to burn off the calories instead of getting rid of them down the toilet, but she'd reacted to that with the same distaste as his earlier query about running or cycling.

She was all about material excess, shiny trinkets and bank balances. He could clearly see how different they were and wondered how he'd ignored it for so long, but he could also see that as long as he could be tempted into a quickie in the car before they arrived at their date location - as had happened about an hour earlier - he would never be able to give her up. He would just have to get used to being the pawn in her world and learning to appreciate the scraps she threw his way.

He overheard someone say that Smaragda had arrived and looked over to the entrance to give her a wave but couldn't see her amongst the crowd.

He had a sudden rush of love for his best friend and was so glad they had found a way to talk about the personal stuff recently. She had always understood him and he knew she would support him no matter what, so this next level of closeness had reinforced his feelings for her and he felt the urge to be close to her and soak up some of that security and safety.

He looked around to find her, thinking that he would confirm their next exercise session, whether it was running or cycling, he didn't mind. Maybe even swimming if he could join her in the morning sometime, but that idea brought to mind the thought of her in a bikini and he was not prepared for the physical reaction that mental image had produced.

He closed his eyes to dismiss that imaginary vision, to open them and find a real life one standing at the top of the staircase in front of him. Was that Jennifer Lopez in a shimmering fitted dress?

She lifted her hand and waved before floating down the steps and he realised with shock that his chunky Jennifer Lopez lookalike of a friend was actually very close to being the exact vision of an extremely glammed up version of the same woman as she appeared in the ballroom scene of Maid in Manhattan.

'Close your mouth, you're catching flies,' she laughed as she stepped in front of him.

'You look beautiful,' he croaked.

'I put on a dress,' she shrugged and he couldn't help but look at her cleavage as it popped under the influence of that simple action.

'I've found our table. Shall we go?' the newly arrived gentleman asked.

'Yes, of course. Stelios, have you met Marinos? He's over from Cyprus for a few days to update us on the new check-in system.'

'Oh, right. Nice to meet you.'

'And you. I think they're about to serve the food so we should get settled in,' Marinos said dismissively.

'Well, I'll see you later,' Stelios assured her.

She smiled and headed for her table, but Marinos gave him the kind of stare which couldn't fail to warn him to keep his distance.

He completely understood. If he'd brought Smaragda tonight, looking like that, he would have been expecting to fight off every other man in sight too, but right at that moment he was so paralysed by an overriding inferno of conflicting emotions that he couldn't move a muscle and simply watched his double chocolate sundae walk away.

SEPTEMBER

Penelope breathed a sigh of relief on hearing the announcement for the German flight departure as she knew she would have a little time before the Austrian passengers checked through and she could take a break from the tills.

She checked her nails and was annoyed to see that the polish was starting to get chipped and was spoiling her faultless appearance. She would have to repair that on her next break as she couldn't stand those kinds of imperfections when she'd taken so much effort to appear as good as she did.

She wandered over to the cosmetic section and inspected the new range of nail varnish which had arrived that morning, in the hope she would find some original shade which would boost her spirit, but was too distracted to really notice anything different.

Her mind was full of the old village house and how she could renovate it to a standard she could be comfortable in. It seemed like a huge job and though she expected Stelios to be happy to make the upgrades, she didn't actually know how far she could push the budget. It was, after all, an overnight escape and he would probably prefer to put more money into a forever home, so she was taking it slowly and trying to gauge his reaction to her ideas. So far, he hadn't seemed interested in anything she had suggested and she'd hoped that was because he was leaving it up to her to make all the decisions, but recently he'd kept reminding her that nothing could be organised until the paperwork was in order and seemed to be brushing her off. She knew it would be a couple of months at least before they could sign the papers, but she wanted to move quickly after that so there really wasn't any harm in getting things ordered in and scheduled so that it would hopefully be ready in time for Christmas and the lavish house warming party she had always dreamed of.

As she thought about Stelios' reaction to her renovation plans, she realised that he really didn't seem as excited as she was about it. She wondered if that was because he wanted to keep some of the original features, as he had obviously been attracted enough to something in that house to buy it in the first place. She knew he was probably a little more old-fashioned than she was, but it really was an old tumble-down kind of place so it needed a total facelift. Once he saw the improvements she had in mind and could picture them both having lazy, sexy nights together, she was sure that he would want to get on with it as quickly as possible.

She smiled to herself because she knew that she had him under her thumb. They'd had sporadic disagreements and more than the odd occasion of feeling as though they weren't on the same page, but as soon as she moved things into the bedroom he just couldn't resist. She'd always had that incredible talent but somehow, when she saw the look of surprise and gratitude on his face, she was sure that she had never before seen anything as delectable. It seemed he wanted her more than any other man she'd ever met and it was an instant aphrodisiac to see total adoration in the eyes of someone who was willing to do anything to please her.

She lost herself for a few moments with images of some of their most successful pairings and tried to dismiss the random downbeat emotions which crept in when she remembered some of the suggestions that he had made to spoil the mood. Their love-making worked because it was all about him showing how much he needed her and the way she allowed him, to a certain degree, into her personal space. Once he started asking for more selfish things and taking the attention away from her, it all became quite tiresome and annoying. She couldn't understand why he wanted to change the routine of what had seemed to be working very well up until that point.

It was possible that he was expecting a bit more from her in repayment for the birthday gift, but she took offence at that because it should have been given freely and he owned half of it anyway. However, when she thought about it a little more, he had started to ask her about going for a swim or a cycle with him and it was sweet that he wanted to spend time together without the sex, but he was way off the mark with what he'd suggested. A holiday in the Maldives, or a shopping trip to New York would be more to her taste or, at the very least, an open-air concert and exclusive hotel in Athens, with a ring as a lasting promise on the last night.

She had dreamed about her perfect proposal, with a huge diamond offered from an irresistibly handsome man, on the rooftop terrace of a top class establishment overlooking a sensational sunset and the knowledge that she would be looked after in an enormous penthouse next to the beach with plenty of sex and money to be enjoyed. Wasn't that every girl's dream?

Stelios was definitely gorgeous enough, but she wasn't sure he could provide the rest of the fantasy so she hadn't thought about it too much recently. Real life was a bit different, but there was no harm in hoping for the best and working towards making it as close to the dream as possible.

Her mood dropped a little at that thought, so she decided to recall a happy moment from her life to lift her spirits again before the next wave of customers appeared.

Without warning, an image appeared in her mind of lying on the beach, covered in bits of sand and sticky lollipop when she had been laughing at something and it had fallen off the stick. Her hair was matted from dipping in and out of the sea and her face was as natural as the day she was born. Her nails were short and unpolished and her tummy was round after sharing a sumptuous picnic. It was the happiest she'd ever been in her life and she smiled broadly.

It wasn't a childhood image of fun and happiness that she had recalled, but a memory of sharing a perfect beach day in Halkidiki. With Shakira.

She was simultaneously overcome with both happiness and horror of how she could enjoy that scenario when it was the total opposite of everything she was trying to be. She'd been reminded of those days by some casual messaging between the two of them, revisiting places they'd been and people they'd met. It had all been quite laidback and insignificant until Shakira had said she was doing a bit of island hopping at the end of the season and would love to catch up.

Penelope hadn't replied as yet, though she had already mentioned Stelios in conversation to avoid any misunderstandings, but she was conflicted over whether to agree and unsure of how she would react if it did happen.

For now, she decided she needed to concentrate on her future with Stelios and move towards making their life together more permanent. If she had to give him a little more attention now and then, she would make the effort as it wouldn't fail to make things better in the long run.

As she heard the new passengers approaching, she moved back to the till area with a smile and resolved to fight off the pull towards Shakira and make Stelios so completely satisfied with her that her every wish would be granted. It was all going to work out perfectly.

Naomi was standing at the front of the queue outside heading for the departures area and she was glad that it gave her a little time to herself instead of having to keep chatting with the guests as they were checking in, or keeping those waiting at the back of the very long line entertained.

There were a few reps around, so she wasn't expected to be the life and soul and, even though Russell wasn't on the rota today, everyone seemed to be satisfactorily occupied.

She would have liked to see Russell at the airport, especially as the Kefalos rep wasn't there as a distraction, but it wasn't the end of the world. They were in an acceptable place for the moment and had somehow moved on from the previous month's spat.

The first meeting after that squabble had been at the airport when her guest had been horribly drunk and of course he had managed to bring the Kefalos rep into a war of words which she definitely didn't need.

She hadn't been able to talk to Russell properly at first because he was kept inside and she was stuck outside trying to chat to the guests but struggling for things to say as her mind was not on the job. Then she'd had to sit with the drunk guest and his wife until he showed he had calmed down and sobered up enough to get on the plane, just before the desk closed. None of the other reps had been around because there were lots of extra arrivals on that flight and they'd had to rearrange coaches and notify resort reps of the changes so they'd been working very closely together and she was upset that she'd missed out on that opportunity.

When she met up with Russell and the others at arrivals, she tried to act like nothing had happened between them and just chatted as naturally as possible.

He reciprocated and everything seemed back to normal, but then he revealed that all the reps knew about their disagreement and it had caused him some problems, so he thought it was better if they just avoided each other for a while to let the dust settle.

She was taken aback because she knew exactly what that meant. There had to have been some truth in her accusation that he was seeing the Kefalos rep and there was nothing she could say because she was standing right there at the other side of the meeting point with a scowl on her face.

She massively regretted her actions, but couldn't beg him to reconsider in such a public place, in front of the person they had argued about and, of course, while they were working. The rest of that transfer and the next few days had been unbearable.

She hadn't meant to start a fight with him at all, far from it, but her emotions had got out of control and his laissez faire attitude had just strengthened her need to know where she stood.

She'd started by suggesting earlier on, during the bar crawl, that they should meet up another night away from work, maybe on the night before his day off? They didn't have the same day off, which had put a spanner in the works for her from the beginning, but she was happy to suffer the happy hangover she thought she'd probably have through work if it meant she'd spent the night with him properly in a one-to-one situation. He'd been very non-committal and said he'd think about it, but that wasn't enough. They were having lots of fun together and clearly fancied the pants off each other, so she just wanted him to take that extra step to wanting to make time to be with her, instead of just making the most of the situation when it presented itself on the nights they were guiding the same trips.

At the end of the night as they'd just enjoyed a quick romp on the beach, she tried another angle and said if he spent his day off there she could meet up with him in the afternoon and they could go to the beach together before she had to go home to shower. She had put plenty of emphasis on the word shower so he would realise he was invited to share it with her and hopefully wait around for second helpings once her duties finished later on.

He almost laughed and said he always went wind-surfing on his day off. It was something he couldn't miss and Kos Town didn't have the right wind currents to do it well.

In that split second she somehow knew that he was going to Kefalos on his day off, because everyone knew that the best place to catch the wind was in its enclosed bay; it was a major attraction. Unfortunately, she was sickened to think that he also considered the rep as a major attraction too and spat out the accusation without thinking.

He'd tried to walk away, saying he didn't need that kind of crap in his life and she needed to grow up.

She'd grabbed him and told him he couldn't spend his time with anyone else when they had such an amazing thing going on between them. All she wanted was to spend a bit more time together.

He reminded her that they hadn't made any promises and they were just having a bit of fun when they got the chance to meet up. He didn't see any problem continuing the way they were, but if she wanted to stop, he would understand.

Although they had returned to the night club where the bar crawl was wrapping up, she continued to shout (even louder to raise her voice above the sound of the beach-pop the DJ insisted on playing) and criticise her rival until she realised a couple of the Kos Town reps were nearby.

She'd hoped they hadn't heard, or at least understood, what was happening, but obviously word had got around since then and if everyone knew about it, then the Kefalos rep also knew and because he'd had some problems due to the information, she could only presume that she was right about everything she had said and they were involved somehow.

He said he'd wanted space to let the dust settle and that could have meant anything, but she hoped it meant he was finishing whatever casual arrangement he'd had in Kefalos and once that was done and dusted, he would come back to her and they could continue.

He didn't attend that week's bar crawl and she wasn't on the Greek night, so the first week was lonely but acceptable. The following week he actually brought two coaches to the bar crawl and was so busy they hardly spoke except for work reasons. At the Greek night it was again busy due to the high season, but they managed a kiss at the end and she hoped that was the start of something new.

Since then they hadn't always been on the same rota, but when they had he'd made an effort to spend ten minutes with her somewhere quiet to catch up and have a kiss and cuddle. There hadn't been any attempt to go any further and she had been surprised, but she presumed this was a new start for them and he was respecting her until they could work out how to proceed.

She was ready to jump into bed with him any time he offered to come over in his free time, but they hadn't got to that point yet.

She presumed he was still going to Kefalos on his day off for the windsurfing, but he could easily do that without seeing the rep and she was generous enough to give her time to get over him as he would definitely be hard to forget.

It would have been nice to see Russell again at the airport, but she knew she would see him soon and she was glad she didn't need to see the sad, sorry face of the Kefalos rep as she probably wouldn't have been able to resist gloating in front of her. Just a little.

'Well done, guys. That was pretty straightforward so go and take a break, then we'll meet up at arrivals,' Mark told them as the last passenger disappeared through Passport Control.

Naomi sat with the girls and enjoyed her drink and mini snack.

'How's it going?' she was asked.

'Yeah, good. What about you?'

'I'm a bit happier now all the crazy Uni kids have disappeared. September's a much calmer month.'

'I know what you mean, but it's a completely different kind of crazy with the all oldies coming in at once. I've never had so many requests for low floors and wheelchair access,' she laughed.

'And they're even worse than the younger ones sometimes. They sit around the pool bar till all hours of the morning and the owners keep complaining that they're keeping everyone awake.'

'Oh, I haven't had that problem, but some of them have swapped rooms, depending on what floor they're on or whether they want the sunshine in the morning or evening. I can't keep up with them,' she sighed. It was nice to have a bit of light banter with her friends.

'They've all booked up for the Greek night, but not so much for the bar crawl. I guess it won't be running much longer.'

'Oh,' Naomi gasped. 'I hadn't thought of that. Maybe enough of the other guests will come and keep it going for another few weeks.'

'Maybe, but it'll probably be better for you if it stops soon. After all that Russell business.'

'Well, it's all sorted out now, so I don't have a problem,' she pointed out determinedly. 'It was a bit embarrassing having it all out in the open, but we're all adults and I'm sure everyone will just carry on now we know where we stand.'

She wasn't particularly comfortable having this conversation, but she was glad that everyone knew about her and Russell and that the other rep was now out of the way. It would mean they could be more open about their relationship and she could try to persuade him to stay over sometime to put things on a more permanent footing.

'That's a good way to look at it. He's not the most dependable person, is he?'

'No, he hasn't been, but I think that… event,' she swallowed hard, 'just brought everything out into the open and we all reassessed what we want. I think he'll be more aware now of how his actions can affect people.'

'I hope so, but I reckon being in his life is going to be like riding a huge roundabout and you'll never know when you're going to get booted off,' the girl laughed rudely.

'I really don't think that's how it is. He's seen the error of his ways and doesn't want to upset anyone else. He wouldn't do that again now,' Naomi said forcefully to convince the other girl, but also herself under the current interrogation.

'Well I'm surprised you're sticking up for him under the circumstances. I mean, he's a good laugh and everything and we've all had a bit of fun with him, but you don't want to go thinking he'll ever be committed, or even faithful.'

'I don't?' she asked as her legs started to shake. Why did this girl think it was OK to tell her that they had 'all' had a bit of fun with him? That was just cruel and, surely, not true?

'Not you, I mean generally. People shouldn't think he'll ever want to settle down. He's just not made that way and if that's something he's promised, I think someone's going to get a massive shock at the end of the season.'

'Really?' she croaked as her voice box tightened up. She hadn't thought about the end of the season at all, but it was actually not that far away and they hadn't discussed what would happen then. She didn't even know if he'd requested any winter work. She hadn't, so she was free to go wherever he might be, but she realised they really needed to make some plans and work out what their next step would be. She didn't want to rush him as he was being very laid back and not discussing his intentions or deeper feelings, but she couldn't be this casual once they left Kos and she decided to make it clear next time they met. It was time they acted like a proper couple and made some plans.

'Yeah, I mean I don't know exactly what he's had to promise to get out of that very awkward situation you all had together,' the girl squirmed at the memory, 'but for everyone to be so calm about it all, he must have really vowed to be totally faithful and never leave resort again, except for work of course.'

'He wouldn't need to do that. He knows what he did was wrong and he doesn't want a repeat performance so he's better off just with one person and he's not going to ruin that happiness for an insignificant liaison with someone it could never work with.'

'Wow! Did he actually say that?' she asked, wide-eyed.

'More or less,' Naomi nodded, though she knew she had only imagined him saying those words to her. Anyway, she knew that was how he felt, so it was about time everyone else found out too.

'God, I don't know if I could cope if someone said that about me.'

'Well, it's the truth so there's no point hiding from it,' she said as she tried to wrap up the conversation. Now that it was all out there, she was happy for word to get around and she wouldn't have to explain any further.

'You're a tough cookie, Naomi,' the girl said as she stood and prepared to move down to the arrivals area.

'Well, I'm happy now, so it wasn't so tough really.'

'But for him to say you had an insignificant liaison, when we all know you were really keen on him... That takes guts to walk away from.'

'Huh?' she asked. That last bit didn't make any sense.

'Yeah. Now he's going to Kefalos at every given opportunity and arranged to be on a different rota to you for the trips, I thought it would be tough for you to live it down and face everyone. But you've really surprised me by being brave and getting on with things, knowing it's all over and he's happy somewhere else. I take my hat off to you, seriously. Now, we'd better get on with these arrivals or Mark will be docking our pay,' she laughed as she left Naomi standing with an open mouth but absolutely nothing to say.

Stelios met Smaragda at the cinema to see the first showing of the latest superhero movie, as had been their habit since childhood.

'No Penelope?' she asked, though she hadn't really expected her to come.

'No, she said she was catching up with friends,' he replied as they joined the queue for tickets.

'Friends? From work?' As far as Smaragda knew, Penelope didn't have any friends. She was always stuck to Stelios like glue.

'No, oh, I don't know,' he shrugged.

'You don't know who her friends are?' How could that be possible?

'I didn't ask. She must have friends I suppose.'

'You've never met them?'

'I don't think so...' he pondered. 'No, I don't think I have.'

'And she's never mentioned them before?'

'She just says she's catching up with them, but I've never asked who they are.'

'Seriously? You've never asked about her friends, who they are, or what they do together?'

'No, it's never crossed my mind.'

'You never talk about what your friends have been doing, or who they're going out with, or where they've been on holiday?'

'No, it's just the two of us and what we've been up to.'

'That wouldn't take long; for you it's running or cycling and for her it's visiting the salon. What else have you got to talk about?'

'We've got better things to do than talk,' he smirked.

Oh, for goodness' sake. Didn't he ever think of anything else?

126

'You really don't just spend time together chatting and relaxing? Don't you miss having the chance to share your hopes and dreams with someone special?'

'That's what you're here for!' he teased as he gave her a nudge.

She was lost for words but was luckily interrupted by the cashier taking their payment and issuing tickets. They wandered over to the counter to choose something to eat and drink then made their way to the allocated seats.

'You've done your hair different,' he noticed as they got comfortable.

'I was due a trim so I got some layers put in. I'm not sure if I like it.'

'It looks nice. Soft.'

'Oh, thanks,' she blushed and was grateful for the low lighting to disguise it.

'It was nice at the Dekapentavgoustos event too, when you put it up. You looked really lovely.'

'Us girls have to make an effort sometimes,' she said breezily, but was starting to feel giddy at such sweet and unexpected compliments. They'd had a few chats at work since that evening, but he hadn't mentioned anything then.

'But you didn't look like a girl that night. You looked much older.'

'Thanks, like a has-been?' she asked uncertainly.

'No, not at all, I meant more mature. You looked like... a woman. A very confident woman.'

He managed to avoid the words gorgeous and sexy because he didn't feel comfortable describing his best friend that way, even though she definitely had been both of those things. Actually, looking at her in this dim light, even without the make-up and tight-fitting dress, she still looked gorgeous. And sexy.

'That's just as well, because I am a woman,' she laughed. She liked the compliments but he wasn't necessarily very good at it.

'Yes, you are,' he said as his smile lingered while he noticed the shape of her own smile on those heart-shaped lips.

'Popcorn,' she asked as she shoved the packet right under his nose. 'The movie's starting so just dive in if you want any more.'

'Right, thanks,' he replied as he was suddenly reminded that he was sitting next to his best friend in the cinema, not his girlfriend, so the thought of leaning in to kiss the salt that was sticking on her bottom lip was definitely not acceptable.

The lights went out and the movie started, but he was too distracted thinking about what had almost happened and how badly she would have reacted. And rightly so.

He could only guess that he was still high from the afternoon session he'd just enjoyed with Penelope in the hot tub at the traditional stone house, which he had rented again to keep the dream alive.

He had practised how to say that it was probably more trouble than it was worth to try to make it good enough to reach Penelope's high standards and they should rethink the idea over the winter. He had been determined to find a way out, but she had presumed they had gone back to have a closer look at the kind of things that would make it perfect and was so overjoyed she had to thank him the only way she knew how. It had been almost a rerun of the first night they had spent there as she was so willing to do anything and everything to keep him happy. They had celebrated energetically and he was once again totally mesmerised by the things she could do with that perfectly toned and flexible body. He was nothing but putty in her hands and even agreed to cancel that evening's outing with Smaragda to the cinema, but his battery was flat and he was secretly happy to keep the appointment as it meant he had some degree of choice in the matter and he really wanted to see that movie.

He'd asked her to come along, but she'd become a little withdrawn and just said she was catching up with friends, so he thought it was a great time to make his escape before the usual let-down of the conclusion of activities set in, as it always did.

He'd managed to keep bright as he'd rushed to get ready and make his way to the cinema, but now his mood was dropping as he realised he had failed to put a stop to the dream renovation.

But there was more to it.

He was also feeling down because he'd just spent an amazing few hours in bed with the most sexy and confident woman he'd ever known, but somehow there was something missing. She had made (almost) all his dreams come true and he really, genuinely had enjoyed every single moment of it. The problem was, now it was over, he didn't feel any better for it. It didn't linger in his mind. He didn't feel like his skin was on fire in the places she'd touched him and he couldn't quite remember what it felt like to kiss her when all the other intense activities had demeaned that simple pleasure.

He knew he was punching above his weight being with Penelope when she could have anyone she wanted with just a look, but even though she had given much more than usual that afternoon and actually paid attention to his needs for a change, he wasn't sure if it was enough.

He couldn't possibly consider being away from her; when would he ever get an opportunity like this again? But when he wasn't actually with her, she didn't stay in his mind and he didn't wonder what she was up to without him. That didn't seem right.

The other thing that didn't seem right was how he had felt the urge to kiss Smaragda in that very strange moment where she had seemed like everything he needed. They were best friends. Buddies. He shouldn't think of her like that. He *didn't* think of her like that.

There must be something not wired properly in his brain. He had been with Penelope for close on a year and she seemed to want to get serious with him, if the house renovation was anything to go by. He should nurture that and be grateful to have struck lucky with such a sensational woman. He didn't need to share all his deepest darkest secrets with her; she wouldn't want to hear them anyway. He could continue to develop his friendship with Smaragda and enjoy the security of knowing she would always support him and offer advice if needed. They had seemed to move into a new level of closeness, so that was a good start for their more mature lives as, no doubt, she would soon meet someone who would love her and treat her in the way she deserved. She was a very special woman who was kind and generous and, yes, beautiful.

He stayed staring at the screen but could visualise that little mole she had on her shoulder. When they were teenagers, she always made sure it was covered up, but when he'd said it made her look glamourous like Jennifer Lopez, she stopped being horrified by it and was happy to let it show as she danced and displayed her J-Lo moves.

He remembered when she'd told him to stay away because her monthly moods had her shouting at everything and everyone, but had been soothed when he suggested ice-cream week and TV movie marathon day.

She still had the scar on her knee from when they'd been climbing trees and the low branch had snapped. He'd never been as scared as when he saw her lying there with pain etched into her face but thankfully she hadn't broken anything, even though she had a large gash which needed several stitches. They'd been fifteen then and he sneaked in through her open bedroom window with two cans of cider to cheer her up, but it had made them throw up and they vowed never to drink it again.

He remembered practising to dye her eyelashes before the school formal and it had all gone wrong. Her eyes had been swollen and red and she'd wept with the pain until he bought some medicated drops to help her recover. She hadn't asked him to help with any of the other preparations after that but on the night of the formal he had been so proud to be her dance partner as she was totally transformed and looked sensational. Her eyes had never looked so bright.

That reminded him of how she had looked at the work's do the previous month. He'd just said she looked 'lovely' but she had looked out of this world. His jaw had literally dropped and she looked so happy and perfect dancing with Marinos. They made a handsome couple but, clearly, he was not good enough for her and wasn't an issue as he'd only been over from Cyprus for a few days.

He'd been delighted to see her so happy and laughing cheerfully, but had experienced a twinge of something that had made him intensely uncomfortable. He thought it was his protective side worrying that Marinos might take advantage. Then he thought that if she had made such a special effort with her hair and appearance to impress Marinos, she would be sadly disappointed when he left and didn't want to think someone could upset her so easily. Then, as he watched them dance, he was suddenly picturing her hips sliding back and forth, without the covering of the dress...

At that point, he had made his way to the bar and downed a couple of Metaxas quickly, before suggesting that he and Penelope left to have some private fun of their own. She had been bored by then and happily went along with his plan so he could escape and stop those ridiculous unwanted thoughts.

Now those thoughts were back again with his unexpected craving to kiss Smaragda's salty lips. Maybe he was just hungry and the salt was too tempting. Maybe he'd been so wrapped up in the hot sex he'd thoroughly enjoyed that afternoon that he simply couldn't shake off that feeling. Maybe he wasn't used to sharing something special with a woman without that physical contact. Maybe, and this was scarily nearer the truth, he felt so comfortable with her, sharing things they loved together, that it was just instinct to lean over and kiss those lips he knew so well, realising that he would finally feel the contentment and satisfaction that he truly needed.

'Oh no!' she whispered loudly as she grabbed his arm as the movie neared its finale. He suddenly felt the heat from her hand burning through his shirt sleeves. 'How is he going to get back now? They've used the last crystal.'

'Don't worry. He'll find a way. He's a superhero,' he

whispered back as he leaned closer to her ear, finding it very hard to move away from her face which was kissably close.

'But they might say to be continued and leave him hanging,' she said anxiously as she turned her face towards him, lips only millimetres apart. 'I just couldn't bear to wait.'

He could feel the breath between them which seemed warm, moist and heavy on both sides. They didn't move for what felt like a lifetime and then she looked up, directly into his eyes and he felt like she had stabbed him through the heart.

'Stelios?' she whispered and her lips just touched the very edge of his as she spoke, sending a wave of fire through him and filling him with a desire that felt so right, but twice as wrong at the same time. She was like his sister!

'Sorry, I need the toilet. Can't wait,' he babbled quickly and shot out of his seat and through the rear doors.

Some time later he got a text message asking where he was and hoping he was OK. He responded that he must have eaten something dodgy that had made him need the toilet so quickly, but he was now at home and resting.

She confirmed the ending of the movie and asked if he wanted her to pop over with anything, or pick something up from the 24-hour chemist, but he said he was just going to go to bed and sleep it off.

She wished him a good night and sweet dreams. He doubted that would be possible for a long, long time.

OCTOBER

Penelope was listening to some music as she prepared for her lunch with Stelios and even dancing to a few of the more upbeat sections.

She'd had a lovely morning and was looking forward to driving out to the next resort of Tingaki, which was about 10km away. There was a lovely quiet road they would take which was parallel to the coastline and every now and again it was possible to spot the neighbouring island of Pserimos and enjoy the gentle motion of the waves between them.

It was a warm and sunny day which, although it could never be guaranteed, was not necessarily unusual for October, so she was wearing a pair of white linen trousers and a light blue blouse with a dark blue wrap stashed in her bag. She felt that it was still summertime, even though everyone at work was talking about the end of the season and how life would get back to 'normal' soon. She wanted to enjoy this sunny and hopeful spell as it would mark the start of something new and lasting. It was only a few days away from her one-year anniversary with Stelios and when he proposed she would be able to talk about all her hopes and dreams for the future.

She wondered if he had any plans of his own, but she couldn't imagine so; men just didn't have the same skill for planning and organising, did they? He would be grateful that she had thought about where they would live and what they could do to improve their job prospects as she recalled how many times they had been frustrated and unsettled by some bad-mannered passengers.

That was, of course, after the big day itself, the thought of which always made her heart race. Oh, she could picture the dress now, even though she hadn't actually found it yet. She'd tried a few on and they had given her ideas, but she hadn't found the perfect shade of white, or the right material and, for some reason, nothing really sat well on her figure to show off her best assets. She'd been disappointed, but not anxious as yet because she knew she had some time. Now that she could actually go ahead and start planning things, it would probably be best to get a stylist to create the perfect dress to her own design. That way she would look perfect as she walked down the aisle and she would know that she would look better than she ever had before and all the attending guests would know it too.

She hadn't thought about which guests would actually be in attendance, but she would want as many as possible to be there so that she could flaunt her happiness and feel the admiration in their eyes. The cake and the music and the flowers weren't as important to her, but she would like a horse-drawn carriage to take her around the town both before and after the ceremony. Generally, newlyweds would drive through the main streets of the town and the driver would sound the horn so that people would be aware and wave their wishes of good luck to the happy couple, but she wanted everyone to see her in her glory at a slower pace where she could register the envy in their eyes.

It was all going to be such a beautiful day to start off a happier and more prosperous life with Stelios. She couldn't wait for it to start and she just had to make sure he understood how important the actual proposal was so that it would be a memory they could share with everyone for years to come. She didn't want to discuss it in detail as that would take away the thrill of the occasion, but she needed to steer him in the right direction so that it would be an unforgettable experience.

Her phone beeped and she saw it was a message from her beloved, saying he was setting off in a few minutes and he would see her soon.

She was about to replace the phone in her bag when she changed her mind with a sly smile and clicked onto her latest chat on Facebook. She read through the comments as she swayed to the music that was still playing and smiled to see the amount of amusing emojis they had both used. It was such a happy, carefree chat and there was obviously still plenty of chemistry between them, but her 'holiday fling' had to stay exactly that and she was beginning to see how she could still have those memories at the same time as forging a new relationship as good friends instead. She had accepted the invitation to catch up as her friend travelled around the islands later in the month, but was sure that her new situation with Stelios would put a halt to any kind of temptation to stray.

She was going to have the chance to get used to having a new name and a new friendship all at the same time and she was really looking forward to this happy development in her life.

She saw Stelios arrive in the street and switched off the Shakira CD before going out to meet him.

'Hello, beautiful,' he said as he opened the car door for her, as usual.

'Hello, yourself,' she smiled and kissed his cheek.

They chatted about the weather, the views and the changing season until they arrived at the restaurant and made themselves comfortable.

'Thanks for sending that hen party group through yesterday. They bought loads of cosmetics, so I had a good day,' she smiled and stroked his hand.

'Hen party?'

'Yeah, they arrived last week and you gave them a leaflet for the duty-free shop.'

'Did I?'

'Yes. They said you went to talk to them when they first arrived and were waiting for their cases; they'd kept hold of the leaflet for when they left.'

'I was on arrivals yesterday, so I didn't see them go through,' he confirmed with some confusion.

'I know, but they'd already seen you last week.'

'Don't remember,' he shrugged.

'You couldn't forget them. They said they were wearing the same stuff for travelling in, so you would remember two thin girls, one fat girl, one black girl and a gay bloke all wearing identical pink tops with their names on.'

'Oh, yes. I do remember now. When I stepped out of the booth after checking everyone through, I found a passport on the floor that belonged to one of them so I had to return it.'

'Well, they definitely remembered you. The gay guy kept saying what beautiful eyes you had and he was sorry you weren't at Passport Control to say goodbye.'

'Yeah, he kept asking what were the best bars to go to and did I want to give them a private tour,' Stelios recalled with a smirk. 'That's why I focused on the women and told them about the make-up and stuff you sell.'

'That's because you are so handsome,' she clucked and pinched his cheek. 'You not only attract the girls, but the boys as well.' She felt a twinge as she remembered having that same effect on both male and female. It was nice but unsettling at the same time.

'Well it's lucky I don't need any extra attention. I've got you,' he nodded in conclusion.

That made her feel guilty, which was not an emotion she was used to. She may have Stelios eating out of her hand, but she knew she needed more than that. It was comforting to have his attention but that wasn't sufficient to stop her from being flattered when others showed their interest. She hadn't been unfaithful and didn't intend to be, so she just hoped that having a ring on her finger would be enough to give her an adequate feeling of achievement, so that other flirtations would become more and more insignificant.

She was reminded of the business at hand and returned to the conversation.

'They seemed happy enough, but I wouldn't be carrying on like that if it was my hen party,' she assured him.

'Well, I guess you don't know till it happens,' he replied automatically, having never thought about that particular event.

'Everyone has an idea of what kind of things they'd like to do,' she laughed condescendingly.

'I don't.'

'But you're not a hen, are you?' she teased.

'Neither are you, officially.' He was bored with this conversation and would rather eat in silence as she sometimes went on and on about things that he had no interest in.

'But the hen party is a big part of the whole wedding package. It's a chance for the bride-to-be to have everyone make a fuss of her and spoil her with lots of lovely treats.'

'I thought it was a chance for her to spend her last night as a singleton with her friends, making pacts to stay in touch in the future? All that girly type of stuff.'

'Well, that as well, but it's mostly about the treats,' she insisted, feeling a little deflated.

'So which female friends would you have at your hen do? You've never talked about any of them before.' He remembered Smaragda's comment and wanted to know if she did actually have any friends hidden away.

'There's all the girls at work! Obviously, I couldn't invite everyone, but they'd all love to be involved if I asked them.'

'Like who?' He asked pointedly.

'You know, Smaragda... and the others. I haven't really thought about it before,' she lied, 'so I haven't actually put a list together or anything.'

'You don't even know their names, do you?' It was just a thought which had somehow made its way out of his mouth, but he hadn't really believed it could be true until he heard it out in the open.

'That doesn't matter.' She waved away his comment

but still felt flustered. This wasn't going as she'd planned. 'It doesn't matter exactly *who* would be there, more the fact that I would be having a much more sophisticated and classy gathering than just going on a cheap boozy holiday.'

'Of course,' he said, as he realised that she couldn't possibly have imagined anything else. It was all about appearances and material goods, nothing to do with friendship and camaraderie.

'I knew you'd understand,' she smiled. 'We always agree about the important things.' She was glad he agreed with her idea of an elegant arrangement and it boded well for what he had planned for the proposal.

'Yeah.' He decided to let it lie as he wasn't in the mood to discuss the importance of an event that was unlikely to happen in the foreseeable future. He would be happy if his fake agreement was an end to that subject.

'Speaking of important things...' she gently brushed his hand again. 'Are we making any plans for Saturday?'

'Saturday?'

'Yes. Have you made any plans for our date on Saturday?' She hated to have to say it out loud, but even if he was trying to keep his proposal a surprise, he would know she would expect to be going out for their anniversary.

'Oh, Saturday, yes, of course.' He suddenly remembered that Smaragda had left a note tucked into his locker to let him know that Penelope had been telling all and sundry that it was their anniversary on Saturday and she was expecting something special. He'd spent more time wondering why she'd left a note and not tried to find him, rather than planning anything 'special' for Penelope.

'Yes, I knew you would have it all planned out, but it's good to know you've got something organised.'

'No problem,' he replied, somehow managing to keep his face expression-free. He had no idea what he was going to arrange for Saturday, but he knew there had to be no way she could misinterpret his actions on this occasion. He'd take her to their favourite restaurant and give her some nice piece of jewellery that would have no strings attached. It would have to be something glitzy and showy, but presumably the lady in the shop would be able to give him some advice.

'Because it's a very special occasion and it won't ever happen again,' she said dreamily.

'What won't happen again?' Did she mean they wouldn't be going out together anymore? The idea really did surprise him as they seemed to have fallen into a regular pattern which he thought she liked, but part of him was a tiny bit relieved that he may not need to keep trying so hard to make it work.

'Oh, well, I mean... um... our first anniversary,' she finally responded. She cursed herself for nearly giving the game away, when he obviously wanted to keep it secret until the night.

'Yes, I see. You're right, you can never relive the first time,' he added sadly. He didn't really mean their first anniversary, as she would suppose, but was referring more to the first times they had slept together. He'd thought his life couldn't get any better and wasn't expecting it to last but now, 12 long months later, he really didn't know if he wanted it to. Her casual comment had struck a chord with him and he could see that they really didn't have anything in common except for the sex and, though he could hardly believe he was admitting it to himself, it just didn't seem enough anymore.

'Exactly. These moments are so precious and will be remembered for years to come. It's important that we treasure each occasion and make them as special as we can so we'll have lots of perfect memories to look back on.' She was sure she had let him know that she was aware of what he was planning and had made it clear that she would be saying yes as long as it was a proposal to remember. 'I'm just going to the rest room to reapply my lipstick.'

As she disappeared to allow time to congratulate herself on handling the situation and give in to the temptation of imagining how perfect it would all be, Stelios sat back and considered the emotions she had just awakened in him.

He was thinking about precious moments that would be remembered for years to come. He was imaging treasuring some occasions which would leave him with perfect memories to look back on. He was repeating Penelope's words, but picturing Smaragda in all those scenes.

He had so many memories with her and there were things he would never, ever, forget.

He smiled at the memory of the day she had opened a yoghurt after lunch in his kitchen and it had sprayed all over her face. She had been miffed, so he flicked a little more on her to make her laugh. She had, but then immediately returned the action and it had developed into a massive food fight with no limits to their resourcefulness. They had landed in a heap on the floor, unable to speak from laughing so heartily at the ridiculousness of their behaviour. She'd had a shower and he'd given her something casual to wear then, when he returned from freshening up, he saw that she'd been cleaning up some of the mess and she'd never looked so at home as she did at that moment, standing there in his kitchen with her wet hair, a mop in her hand and wearing his clothes.

It was the smallest of moments, but it was something he would never forget as long as he lived. She just looked so perfect and like she couldn't belong anywhere else. He felt full of love for her and, for once, was not uncomfortable to have that emotion.

He'd been thinking about her a lot since their near-kiss, when he'd escaped in a haze of disgust and confusion. He'd spent a good while believing that it was wrong to feel that way and he had avoided her at work as much as possible, except for a quick 'good morning' or a little wave.

He was sure she hadn't realised he wanted to kiss her because she hadn't referred to it at all, though he wasn't sure why she hadn't chased him up before now as they hadn't been out for run or cycle since then. There had been a few rainy or windy days, which they would have avoided anyway, but it was strange how their regular exercise had just stopped at that point. He'd thought it was for the best though, as he didn't know if he could be around her and still fight off those feelings.

He suddenly felt relief at being able to have those feelings without being disgusted by himself. He'd always loved Smaragda and he'd thought they were friends, but now he realised with an overriding sense of inevitability that he loved her in the way that a man was supposed to love a woman. Completely, totally, heart and soul. He loved her with every cell of his body and it had reacted urgently enough times when she was around to be sure of that. But he also loved their connection; they didn't even have to speak to know what was on the other's mind. One look from her would tell him exactly what she was thinking and he was usually thinking the same thing. They had the same views on everything and they could laugh at such ridiculous stuff that no one else would have understood. She was exactly what he wanted, needed and deserved in his life and he knew he could be the same for her. He knew he'd always loved her and was glad that his brain had finally woken up to that fact so he could act on it.

'Thank you, sir.' The waiter interrupted his thoughts as he returned the bill with his change.

Stelios was brought back to earth with a thud. He was taking Penelope out for their one-year anniversary in a couple of days. He couldn't just break up with her now and he couldn't just switch from one to the other. What if Penelope caused a scene and made things difficult at work? What if Smaragda didn't love him? How could he live with giving up regular and amazing sex if things didn't go his way? What if Smaragda didn't love him? Would he be better to end things before the anniversary, or give Penelope one last 'moment' to remember? What if Smaragda didn't love him? How was he ever going to explain why he so suddenly didn't want to continue in the relationship?

What if Smaragda didn't love him?

'Ready to leave?' Penelope asked as she returned to the table.

'Definitely,' he replied. He just didn't know if he was strong enough to do it.

'OK guys, same deal every time,' Mark told the reps as the last guests disappeared through to Passport Control. 'Do what you've gotta do and meet me at the other side in ten.'

'I can't believe we'll be doing this for the last time next week,' the rep with excessive make-up said.

'I know. How did it get to the end of October so fast?' Naomi wondered.

'We were having too much fun to notice!'

'Yeah, that must be it. I haven't really got my head around the idea of going home yet.'

'Hey, hang on there a minute. We've still got a week to partayyyy,' the rep wiggled and laughed, along with everyone else.

'I know, but it seems to suddenly just be here and there are so many things I didn't get to do,' Naomi moaned.

'Then you'll just have to come back next year and do it all again!'

'Sounds good,' Naomi replied as they all dispersed to do whatever they individually needed to do before moving over to the arrivals hall.

Did it really sound good though? She was right when she said she hadn't done lots of things she'd wanted to and there were places she hadn't seen properly, but would she really want to come back the following year if Russell was back too?

After she had discovered the truth so bluntly last month, she had been an absolute wreck. For the first time that season she didn't give a speech on the arrival coach about the layout of the island and all the amazing things the guests would have a chance to do. She didn't talk about the kind of food they might want to discover, or the sites of historical ruins around the town they could access free of charge. She didn't even warn them about the sun still being capable of sunburn at that time of year, or how they absolutely, without fail, every single time, had to put the paper in the bin and not down the toilet.

She knew that if she opened her mouth to say more than a few words she would dissolve into hysterical tears from which there'd be no recovery.

She'd got through the arrivals procedure in a state of shock as she hadn't fully understood what she'd been told, but slowly pieced together what she'd heard that day with how Russell had been acting since their altercation and realised it was actually, really, honestly, true.

She thought he had stayed distant because he was showing her respect and not pushing her to get intimate with him while she had to get over his deceit with the Kefalos rep. She believed that they were letting the dust settle, as he put it, and starting slowly again so that they could create an equal and long-term relationship. She knew he was a very physical person and she suspected he was really struggling to keep his hands off her and she fell for him even harder because of that, almost giving in several times and wanting to initiate something herself.

Once the truth was out, she'd had to accept that he had never actually explained anything to her and she had just presumed she understood his actions, based on how she felt about him. She'd told the guests that she had a sore throat and was resting it so that she could talk to them properly at the welcome meetings the next day so she managed to drop them all off without getting involved in any deep communication and then went home and cried herself to sleep.

Since then, the bar crawls had dried up and she had never been on the same rota as him for the Greek Night, which ate at her for a while and then she realised it really was over so she didn't want to see him in that environment anyway as it would just hurt too much.

They did occasionally meet up at the airport, but didn't engage in any meaningful conversation and when she was on the same flight as the Kefalos rep they managed to avoid each other completely.

Today was the biggest flight of the week and there were quite a few reps on duty, including Russell and his *girlfriend*. She couldn't bear to describe her like that, but it was true and she had accepted it, even though the pain still remained.

She wandered up to the arrivals area as she was bored of waiting around on her own, but realised too late that she should have taken her time when she heard the Kefalos rep chatting to one of the others about, naturally, Russell.

'He's really romantic though,' she said, noticing Naomi's arrival but not including her in the conversation. To her credit she didn't raise her voice to make a point, so that was something.

'Really?' the other rep queried as she rolled her eyes in disbelief.

'Yeah, he's all the big man in front of everyone else, but when we're on our own he's really sweet and caring.'

'He can be sweet, I guess.' It was at this point that Naomi realised the rep who was receiving this information was the one who'd admitted to being taken in by Russell the previous year and had been sure to stay out of his way since then.

'Absolutely. He's got a reputation for being a bit of a

boy, but he's settled down now and we've had some really lovely times together.'

Naomi wanted to move away, but it would be obvious why and she didn't want to give *her* the pleasure of seeing that she'd won.

'He was always one for a good time,' the other girl agreed.

'But he's grown up now and he's had a change of heart this summer. We've really connected and found something pretty special.' She paused for effect. 'He said I'm his favourite distraction.'

Naomi felt her stomach thud in exactly the same way as it had many months ago when she'd overheard that same voice say that Russell had told her his assignation with Naomi had been a mistake.

"My favourite distraction" had been what he'd called her when they had slipped away from the action to have some time on their own. She felt sick, hurt, jealous and, actually, pretty bloody angry!

'Better than being called his favourite shag, I guess,' the other girl laughed.

Naomi wasn't sure if she meant that as a joke or if it was something Russell had called her during their time together the previous year.

'Who says he hasn't said that too?' the Kefalos rep winked.

Clearly, she hadn't picked up on the other rep's reason for saying that phrase, but it proved Russell used the same lines with all his conquests. His current girlfriend obviously thought she was getting the full treatment but Naomi could see, quite plainly now, that she was just the latest in a very long line.

'Well, good luck to you,' the other rep said half-heartedly and seemed to want to shut down the conversation as she could see Naomi hovering in the background.

'We don't need luck. We're both going to Cyprus this winter so we might end up staying over there all year round. It would be a great place to settle down.'

That last comment really stung Naomi and her belief that Russell and this latest fling didn't have a strong relationship, which had taken over from her momentary anger, was now replaced with that reliable favourite, jealousy.

'Ugh, not for me. I'm happy in Kos and I couldn't dream of being anywhere else.'

'That's good to hear,' Mark said as he appeared with some of the other reps and started handing out the arrival sheets.

They were all organised into duties for arrivals, taxis, walkway and coach park and Naomi was particularly grateful that the Kefalos rep was out of the way near the coaches. Unfortunately, she was working in the same area as Russell which brought a mixture of emotions out in her, but common sense won out and she knew that, in time, she would get over him and find someone better. It wouldn't take much to be better than Russell, after all.

She saw him turn on the charm with the arriving guests and realised it was his default mode. When she'd first seen it in action up close at the welcome dinner, she'd thought it was just for her and she had swooned when he'd switched it on ever since. Now she could see it was just his way with everyone; he had that talent of making whoever he was speaking to feel as though they were the only person in the world and they were always completely won over by being the focus of his attention.

She didn't regret spending time with him because, as the girls had said, he was a lot of fun, but she shouldn't have got so wrapped up in him and missed out on all the other opportunities she could have experienced instead.

She could only imagine how the Kefalos rep's life would be from now on. She might think she had Russell to herself, but it would only be a matter of time until he wanted something new. She would be spending every minute looking over her shoulder, wondering where he was when they were apart and watching the clock until he returned. He probably wouldn't put up with rotas being arranged so he was never on duty with other female reps and that would be just the start of it.

She had been jealous over what she had heard and the thought of Russell and his girlfriend being happy together in Cyprus while possibly planning to stay there long term. She was a little upset that the life she wanted with him had been granted to someone else and it still ached to give up what she had hoped for.

Things might work out for the two of them, they might not, but Naomi was sure that it wouldn't be straightforward for either of them and she was finally glad to know she wouldn't be the one in that position, facing that uncertainty.

There would be no more doubting how someone felt about her, or wondering what they were doing on their day off, or trying to sneak those brief special moments into a guiding duty. She would never be in that situation again because she'd been badly burned and she would be more careful next time.

Next time. That made her smile.

Smaragda was glad to be finishing her shift. It had been a busy day and she was ready for a hot chocolate and some muffins as she read her latest paperback thriller in bed.

Tomorrow was the last day for package holiday flights and then everyone would be able to relax a little more and the continuing domestic flights were spaced out enough to bring a sense of calm to the airport for a change.

She sincerely hoped they would make an effort in the coming months to finish the extension they had been building outside for the last couple of years, as it was supposed to help everything run much more smoothly and that would definitely be welcomed.

She wished she could make her life run a bit smoother too, but as she wasn't running or cycling anymore and the swims would be ending soon with the colder temperatures, she felt like a real life Bridget Jones with her weight starting to increase and spending her time listening to sad songs on the radio.

She knew exactly when it had gone wrong and she badly wished she could rewind time and change what had happened. What had nearly happened.

The longer Stelios had been dating Penelope, the more she realised she had feelings for him which exceeded the friendly banter they'd had growing up together. She was surprised and tried to dismiss her attraction as he would have been horrified to think she considered him that way. It had been hard, but he was obviously in love with Penelope and they had developed a serious relationship together so she had to accept that they would only ever be friends.

A couple of times when they were out running together, he'd brushed against her and she had enjoyed the sensation, finally giving in to her feelings while knowing nothing could ever come of it. She had appreciated the view when he had cycled in front of her and treasured the accidental touching of hands as he passed her the water bottle. She hadn't expected the strong physical connection when he wrapped her towel around her shoulders as they dried off after a lovely morning swim and she had selfishly leaned into him as though she was keeping warm to prolong the moment for a few, very pleasant, extra seconds.

She knew it was not a romantic relationship they had, but in those few moments she had allowed herself to imagine what it might be like to share that with him and she had loved the thought of always having him in her life, whoever he was dating.

She would obviously never tell him how she felt because he didn't see her like that and she would never get in the way of his relationship as long as he was happy, but she couldn't imagine ever loving anyone else so she would just have to get used to being good friends and enjoying any private moments they might share along the way.

One of those 'private moments' had been her undoing when they had gone to the cinema together. She spent the whole time on edge, being so close to him in the dark, especially after he'd given her some compliments about her hair and how she'd looked on a work's night out.

She'd stuffed herself full of popcorn to stop herself from saying anything obvious, but she was so nervous sitting next to him with their arms almost touching all the way through the movie that she realised she had no choice but to own up and reveal how she felt. She wished it had been a scary movie so that she could snuggle into him like they had done in the past but a superhero movie, though one of her favourite genres, was not really one to be scared of. Then she struck lucky near the end of the movie where the hero was in danger and, before she had thought how to proceed, she had grabbed his arm and expressed her fear. She felt the rush of lightning through her hands as the heat from his body surged through his shirt sleeves and into the palm of her hand. She almost jumped back with the sensation, but it was such a strong jolt with such an intense heat, she immediately believed he was feeling the same as her and he seemed to confirm that as he leaned in to whisper calming words into her ear.

The next moment had stayed in her mind ever since. They'd stared into each other's eyes, long and hard and she had said his name as she moved to kiss him. It was inevitable.

Unfortunately, she had her bag beside her and it had stopped her from leaning any further forward so she had just remained there with her lips pouted and ready for action.

He'd glared at her in surprise and probably horror as he'd instantly made his excuses and run out of the theatre!

She had been appalled at her behaviour and terrified she had made the biggest mistake of her life. She sat in shock as the film ended and then realised she had to face the music. She had to apologise for what had happened and make some kind of excuse as to why she had acted that way; maybe she could say she was swept up in the film and was living out a scene where she was with the hero?

She knew that sounded lame, but if she admitted she had tried to kiss him, whatever excuse she gave would still leave the fact that she had wanted him in that moment just hanging in the air. Neither of them could continue their friendship after that because he wouldn't be comfortable around her and she wouldn't be able to speak without watching everything she said.

She'd sent a general message asking if he was alright, so that she could test the water beforehand. When he replied quickly that he'd eaten something dodgy and was going to rest she didn't know if he was just making something up to spare them both, or if he really was ill by strange coincidence. She'd asked if he needed anything from the chemist, but he said he would sleep on it and nothing else was mentioned.

She presumed she'd been mistaken and he hadn't understood what she had been trying to do and that he really had just become suddenly ill. She was glad for that, but felt guilty about the intense heat from his arm which she'd interpreted as being a relentless passion when it was obviously a symptom of his food intolerance.

Since then she'd had to reassess her belief as he had been quite distant in the following days. He was very polite through the few messages they'd exchanged but he didn't go out of his way to see her at work and she realised that he really had understood what she had done, but was trying to save them both the embarrassment of bringing it out into the open.

She'd decided to stay away from him to avoid any difficult conversations and they had since continued to be friendly on the surface but she was torn up inside by the fact she had lost not only her best friend and her exercise buddy, but possibly also the love of her life.

She felt it especially strongly this week as she had heard on the grapevine that, when Stelios and Penelope had gone out for their anniversary meal, things had not gone to plan and there had been some shouting and smashing of plates.

She wanted to go to him and offer her support, although she presumed everything was back to normal as he seemed to be manning his post with his usual carefree attitude. She hadn't seen Penelope in a few days, but that could mean she wasn't on the same rota or, most likely, she was having some days off to avoid the gossip that such an embarrassing scenario would produce.

She was desperately sad that she had lost a good friendship with Stelios over one stupid mistake. She wished she had just kept her sentiments to herself and she would still have a good friend, a way to experience those true love feelings and some kind of life.

She would never make that mistake again as she would never get close enough to anyone else to let them in.

NOVEMBER

Stelios took his cup of hot tea over to the table that was nearest to the heater in the canteen as the temperatures had dropped remarkably in the last few days. He put the unopened envelope down on the table in front of him and wrapped his hands around the ceramic warmth for comfort.

He wasn't sure he wanted to know the contents of that half-expected message as he had been avoiding the truth for the last couple of weeks and had eased into a bubble of safety, where the world and all its problems couldn't penetrate.

He believed that when he opened the letter and read the contents, he would regret having been so open with his feelings in trying to bring about a change. It would have been a shock to hear him say those words and, as there had been no further update until this letter, it didn't seem as though his declaration had been accepted.

He toyed with the idea of leaving the letter for another day, but thought that if he could remember exactly what had been said between them, he might have more of an understanding what it was she actually wanted to say.

It had all started on the night of his and Penelope's anniversary, when they'd arrived by taxi at their regular favourite haunt.

'Oh, we're starting here then?' She'd asked in a tight voice.

'Yes, we always love it here so I thought it would be the best choice.' He hadn't been in a great mood and he was having problems pretending to care when he now knew that he really, really, didn't.

'Hmm. Well, it'll do for a start.'

He didn't know what that meant as he'd planned to get through the meal then complain of stomach pains and make his excuse to leave before there was any chance that they'd have to get physical. It wasn't something he could imagine with those newly recognised feelings for Smaragda tugging at his heart.

They'd gone through the motions of ordering and eating their favourite dishes and were finishing the wine when Stelios decided he just couldn't fake it anymore and had to leave as soon as possible.

'Oh, here's your anniversary present,' he said as he passed her a small, but fancy, bag from one of the unique traditional shops in the old town.

'What's this?' she said with a look of horror.

'You're present,' he shrugged. He wanted to add that he was sorry it wasn't another small house to match the other, but realised he should say as little as possible if he wanted to keep things calm.

'No,' she replied and passed it back.

'What? You don't want it?' he asked with complete surprise. Refusing a gift was unheard of for Penelope.

'Not here. You need to give it to me when we get to the right place,' she hissed, as though she thought other people were listening.

'What place? To be honest, I'm not feeling great. I might have to call it a night,' he told her, grabbing any opportunity to get away quickly.

'You can't!' she squealed with a look of extreme annoyance. 'You have to do it properly.'

'Do what? I'm not kidding, I can't hang around. Either open your gift or don't, but I need to leave.'

He'd started to stand up but she had grabbed his arm and held him there with a strength borne out of desperation.

'You will sit here and do it properly. I can't believe I'm stuck in this ordinary place without a glass of champagne in sight, but if you're going to give it to me here it'd better be worth it.'

He had no idea what was wrong with her and no idea what 'doing it properly' had to do with anything, but it seemed that she wanted her gift to be presented with some kind of exhibition, so if that's what it took to get away from there, he would do his best.

'Happy anniversary Penelope,' he said as he presented the bag like it was the rarest of diamonds, though he was unable to utter any loving entreaties.

'Get it out!' She demanded through clenched teeth. 'Offer it!'

'Wha… Oh, for goodness' sake,' he exclaimed as he finally lost his patience and tipped the bag over to let the box fall onto the table. The edge of it caught on some tomato puree which had slipped off one of their plates.

He held out the box and offered it to her.

'What are you doing?' she asked in a very matronly

voice. 'You're spoiling everything. Take the ring out and get down on your knee. Now.'

'What ring? What the hell are you talking about?'

By that point, everyone in the restaurant had been looking at them because there was obviously something unusual going on.

'My engagement ring. I know what you're doing, but you need to do it properly Stelios, or I'll never forgive you for this,' she warned menacingly.

'Engagement ring? Are you kidding?' he laughed and opened the box to show a fancy piece of costume jewellery which could be worn round the neck. Once he'd decided he couldn't continue much longer with Penelope, he had realised anything remotely expensive would give the wrong impression and be a complete waste of money. He knew she wouldn't be best pleased with a cheapish trinket, but the fact that she expected an engagement ring was totally out of his comprehension.

'What the hell is *that*?' she screamed. 'Where is my ring?'

'That's your gift and there is definitely no ring,' he replied plainly and definitively.

'How can you do this to me, after everything I've done?'

'Wait a minute, after everything *you've* done? What's that supposed to mean?' His temper might not be at quite the same heights as hers, but it was definitely rising.

'I've been going out of my way to make you feel special, knowing you were about to propose and make things official.'

'So, hang on... All that... recently,' he couldn't discuss the current change in their sexual dynamics in a crowded restaurant, but he was not going to take her comment lying down, 'was just because you thought I was going to propose?'

'Of course. I didn't mind putting in the extra effort then, but now I know it was for nothing I feel used, Stelios. You owe me!'

'I owe you?' he fired back. Now he really was angry.

'Yes, you should be doing everything you can to make me feel special and providing a secure start for our future together.'

'I don't believe this,' he sighed and dropped back in his chair. 'I never stopped making you feel special; everything was on your terms and I just went along with it, doing my best to keep you happy.'

'So why ruin it now? At the most important moment? Where is the ring that I deserve?'

'Honestly? I don't know,' he shrugged. He hadn't expected the evening to end up that way, but now the truth was out he couldn't pretend any longer. He would have to tell her it was over and that would be that.

'Then you'll have to find it,' she declared as she sat back in her chair to mirror his movement. They stared across the table like rivals playing Russian roulette.

'We're not getting engaged.'

'Yes, we are.'

'You can't seriously expect us to commit to each other after that bizarre revelation?'

'That's exactly what I expect. We've been going along perfectly well until now. I'm not going to throw away a relationship I've been working on for a year just because you dropped the ball at the most important stage.'

'You've been 'working' on our relationship? Since when?'

'Since the beginning. And now it's your turn to put some effort in. You'll have to really pull the stops out if you expect me to forgive you for this monstrosity,' she threatened as she pushed the abandoned gift box away with annoyance. Unfortunately, it knocked over a glass which fell on the floor and smashed.

Neither of them moved; neither did the waiters who were staying back and keeping out of it.

'You can't, seriously, still expect me to buy you a ring? Are you crazy?'

'I must have been, to think you knew how to do this properly. I'll give you one more chance if you can start to learn how I expect things to be done.'

'I don't need another chance. This can't possibly work.'

'I know you think you don't deserve my forgiveness. I'm not sure you do really, but I'm willing to try to forgive you if you make the effort. I'm doing all the work here and you really need to step up.'

'This is ridiculous. I'm leaving now,' he said as he tossed a few notes from his wallet on the table and headed for the door.

'Not without me,' she declared, hot on his heels, forcing him to pause in the entrance hall.

'What do you want from me? Because I can't give it to you.'

'But you can learn,' she implored. 'All you need to do to put this right is to arrange a spectacular evening with a proper celebration and proposal and then we can find a way to help you improve your other skills.'

'That's never going to happen.'

'It will. I'll help you. Once the renovations have been done, we'll be well on the way to a happy future where you'll be much more able, in all sorts of ways.'

'No, I mean the evening you want can't ha... Wait, are you talking about the renovations to the house in Asfendiou?'

'Of course, our little love nest.'

Now was his chance.

'Well, I'm not buying it. Never was. You got the wrong end of the stick and I just went along with it. It's not even for sale. Thanks for being so grateful though. That really was an experience,' he smirked with the relief of getting it off his chest once and for all.

'What do you mean?' she asked in total confusion.

'I mean I haven't bought the house and don't intend to. Apart from anything else, I couldn't possibly afford it.'

'But you said it was all ours to enjoy on a romantic getaway...'

'No, I said it was all ours, but I meant for just that one evening. When you were so happy to think I'd bought it and thanking me so generously, I was having too good a time to be honest about your mistake, but I can be honest now. It's not ours and it never will be.'

'I can't believe it. You lied to me for so long. All that time...'

'I know and I'm sorry, but I just didn't know how to tell you.' He spoke more calmly because her face had crumpled into something unrecognisable. He thought she would be furious, but she seemed genuinely upset and he hadn't expected that.

'It was going to be a dream home, my romantic escape hideaway.'

'Well, that just proves how wrong you got me. I'm not the person you want to be with. You need someone who can give you those things.' He hoped she would accept the break up without too much fuss once she understood that he wasn't what she had thought.

'That's just unacceptable,' she replied as her shoulders shook and the tears started to flow.

He'd never seen her cry and didn't know how to react. He instinctively put his arms around her shoulders and she folded into him as naturally as she usually did.

She sobbed for a while and he gave her some comfort as he wanted their last time together to be kind rather than angry.

They moved outside to the waiting taxis and it was an unspoken acceptance that they would be travelling separately so he stepped back to allow her to take the first one.

'I'm sorry I lied about the house and that I told you in a harsh way. I could have done it better.'

'Yes. That wasn't fair and it hurt. It's going to take a while to come to terms with that.'

'I'm sure with a bit of time you will come round and feel ready to move on.'

'Time, yes that's what I need,' she said as he opened the car door for her, as usual.

'And then everything will look much better,' he said in conclusion, with a kiss to her cheek.

'I hope so. Having a break is definitely what we need right now. I'll be in touch when I've thought things over and we can decide where we go from here. As long as we're totally honest with each other in the future we'll be much happier and able to look forward to a long life together.'

She smiled sadly and closed the door.

The taxi had driven away before he had even processed what she'd said and he was left with a feeling of having climbed a mountain to find he was all alone in the silence of the clouds with no view whatsoever.

Now here was the letter and he couldn't open it.

He had no choice if wanted any chance of being with Smaragda. He had to face what Penelope had written, then find a way to convince her that he didn't love her anymore and confirm that their relationship was over. He couldn't do anything else until that was finalised and he was free to declare his love to Smaragda. If she didn't feel the same way, he would have to accept it and try to repair their friendship instead, because he couldn't bear to have a life without her in it.

He tore open the envelope with determination.

Stelios, I hope this note finds you well.

A lot has changed since we last spoke and I owe you an explanation which is long overdue.

As you know, I arranged to take some holiday leave to think things over. Initially, I was planning to stay at home and sulk over our argument, but I got the opportunity to do a little island hopping, so I grabbed the chance and have been having some fun in lots of beautiful marinas, beaches and villages all around Greece.

This has opened my eyes to what I really want from my life.

Before we met, I had some free time where I travelled and had many amazing experiences and met lots of very unique people who really brought out the best in me. I hope you don't mind me saying, but it was the best time of my life.

When we got together, I thought I was growing up and doing the right thing to stay on the island where I was born and settle down with a life partner. I hoped that was you.

I think we had a good time at the beginning, but as the months passed it seemed like I couldn't quite hit the highs I'd experienced when I'd been free to behave in any way I wanted, with all those like-minded people around me. I didn't fully recognise it at the time, but I see now that I was trying to make everything in my life the best it could be, whether that was myself, my job, my boyfriend, my relationship or my home. I just had to make everything better and better to feel the same rush I did when I had the freedom to be the real me and I could behave in a way that just wasn't possible in my home town.

I once heard someone call me a perfectionist. They were probably right, but nothing I did ever seemed to reach the point of perfection. It was never quite enough. You weren't quite enough. I wasn't quite enough.

Nothing was ever going to be enough unless I could find the girl I used to be and release her into a world where she was comfortable and at peace with herself.

I don't know if this is making sense to you, so I shall just say that, finally, I am in the place I want to be and I am so unbelievably happy to be the person I want to be. The person I've always been – inside.

I am now free to enjoy my life and my future is looking rosy.

I hope you are not too disappointed, as I now understand you were not ready to commit, so have lots of fun and maybe one day you will get to that point. I hope so.

Take care and know that even though we weren't meant to be, I will always treasure the memory of the tree where you carved our initials. P + S will always be special to me.

Pen x

Stelios took a deep breath and reread the letter. There were so many things he didn't really comprehend: the 'real' her, the 'person' she wants to be, being 'free' to enjoy her life. What did it all mean? And who had ever called her Pen?

The 'perfectionist' part he could understand; she did always push and push to make things better when he was quite happy as they were. He felt that he could probably accept her reason for going to those extremes, but he'd had no inkling whatsoever that it came from a place of unhappiness or inadequacy and he was sad about that.

In the end, he'd had exactly the outcome he wanted and if that meant Penelope was happy in her new life away from Kos, then that was better for both of them.

He opened his phone and sent Smaragda a message asking if she was free for a drink tonight. He simply couldn't wait any longer.

As he left the canteen, he picked up the postcard that Penelope had enclosed for the staff and pinned it on the noticeboard. It was a beautiful scene of a very picturesque beach and, even though he had a hard time imagining Penelope having any kind of fun while getting covered in sand, he hoped she was as happy as she sounded on the message she had written:

HAVING THE TIME OF MY LIFE IN HALKIDIKI!

Elias opened the boot and extracted the suitcases, while Mark retrieved the hand luggage and extras that had been crammed in the back of the car alongside Zoe and Jane.

They'd spent an extra couple of weeks enjoying the peace and quiet of the place they loved once the tourists had left, but now it was their time to depart and they were staying overnight in Athens as an additional treat.

'All good things come to an end, eh?' Elias laughed as he slapped Mark on the back.

'Not an end, just a break,' Mark insisted. 'We'll be back before you know it.'

'No, I will know it next time,' he assured them with a little embarrassment. 'I will check your details carefully.'

Mark laughed at the fact that Elias still remembered being asleep in bed when they had first arrived, although he hadn't laughed then.

'I know you will,' he responded, not bothering to correct the misunderstanding. 'Come here.'

'Oh, yes,' Elias smiled as he was hugged like a brother. 'Good travels to you all.'

There were a few more hugs and slightly quivering lips from Jane before Elias left the airport and they proceeded inside.

'Well, here's a friendly face to see us off,' Mark smiled as he walked up to the desk to check in with Smaragda.

'You're leaving?' she asked unnecessarily, but as was custom in these situations.

'Yes, we're going back through Athens so we can spend another night there before we go back home.'

'That sounds nice. There's lots to do there if you have the chance for a longer visit another time.'

'Oh, that's a fantastic idea,' a voice volunteered from behind them.

They turned to find Stelios standing awkwardly with a large bunch of flowers and turned back to see Smaragda beaming with delight and blushing at the same time.

'Wait a minute,' Mark smiled cheekily, as he pointed his finger back and forth. 'You two?'

'Yes,' Stelios announced with a grin that outshone them all.

'Well isn't that nice? Congrats to you both. Of course, everyone knows Kos is the island of love, I mean, look at us!' he said as he pulled Zoe in for a kiss.

'Hello? Gooseberry!' Jane reminded them.

'Oh, don't worry Jane. Love will find you; just wait till next year, you'll see,' he announced.

'Or we'll find it for you,' Zoe promised.

'Time to go I think,' Jane instructed as they dropped their suitcases off and made to head for the domestic departure gate.

'Let's leave these lovebirds to it,' Mark said as he allowed Stelios through to deliver his flowers to a still-beaming Smaragda.

'Kalo Taxidi. Have a good trip and we'll see you next year,' she called after them.

'See you next year. Have a good winter and take care of each other,' he replied.

'That's exactly what we'll do,' Stelios confirmed as he moved in to kiss Smaragda now that everyone had disappeared.

Kalo Taxidi.

Thanks for reading this episode of the Aegean Sun series. If you'd like an exclusive FREE short story entitled The Zia Sunset Excursion, simply request it by adding your email address to the message on the 'contact' page of my website.

As I'm sure you know, word of mouth is crucial for any author to succeed, so if you have enjoyed **Aegean Sun: The Airport** please consider leaving a review at Amazon, even if it's only a line or two; it would make all the difference and I would be very grateful for your support.
Thank you xx

AUTHOR'S NOTE

In this episode of the Aegean Sun story, I was drawn to use the airport as a base to explore the lives and loves of the different people who pass through it during the summer season.

Some travellers view the airport as a stage to endure until they can reach their destination, but others enjoy every minute of their holiday from the moment they present their ticket and passport at the check-in desk.

Whether you begin your holiday on the morning of your departure, or only once you arrive at your destination, everyone passes through the same airport on their journey and it forms a significant part of that experience.

When I was working at Kos airport on changeover days, I was interested to see how the passengers and the staff held quite a different view of the airport; the first group were waiting around for a limited amount of time, while the second were kept very busy for the whole of the day. I wondered how that affected their opinion of the place and how their private lives were influenced by the occasional unexpected events.

I hope reading this book has given you a reason to smile so that next time you pass through the airport (especially if it is in Kos) you will remember the behind-the-scenes effort which has gone into making it a valuable part of your holiday.

As ever, I am always interested in hearing about any of your holiday experiences and you can reach me on most social media outlets, details of which can be found on my website: www.stephaniewood.co.uk

Happy reading,
Stephanie

OTHER BOOKS IN THIS SERIES

ROOM 101
follows the antics of the holidaymakers in that room of
the Aegean Sun hotel

THE AFTER EFFECTS
reveals what happens when some of those
holidaymakers return home

THE DIARIES
of Mark, the rep, who doesn't hide his feelings

ROOM 102
follows some more holidaymakers a year later, some
returning from Room 101

THE OFFICE
reveals what the reps in the office have to deal with

THE WEDDING
shows Kos out of season for a Greek celebration with
visiting Brits

ROOMS AND REVELATIONS
more fun from the holidaymakers and hotel staff
another year later

THE HIGH STREET
diversifies to locals who work in Venizelou Street, off
Eleftheria Square

A PAIR OF SUMMER SHORTS
Two short stories featuring Eleni the cleaner and Athena
the guide

THE AIRPORT
explores the lives and loves of the people passing
through the airport

THE KAFENION
takes a look at the personal lives of visiting customers
and staff at the café

GRACE'S STORY
reveals the truth behind the secret romance discovered
in The Kafenion – spoilers!

OTHER BOOKS BY THIS AUTHOR

CHRISTMAS ON THE CLOSE series:

The First Christmas
Imogen has her own ideas about what makes a perfect Christmas day and she is pulling out all the stops to make it as delightful as a dream. Can Richard solve the problems that threaten to derail the festive season and stop them from turning her dream into a disaster?

The Christmas Cracker
Paul has grown close to Tricia's son and - from the outside - they seem like a content little family, but will Jacob ever treat him like a real dad?
Why is the man who abandoned her seven years earlier now trying to worm his way back into Tricia's life and will she be tempted to give their relationship a second chance?

A Festive Temptation
Patrick is happy to let Joss take the lead and organise his social calendar, without realising that the arrangements are not always mutually beneficial.
When an unscheduled encounter leads to the suggestion of a new experience, Joss has to decide if she is prepared to stretch the rules but would she, in actual fact, be breaking them?

Countdown to Christmas

Recently-retired Ray is at a bit of a loose end and is looking for something rewarding to fill his time so that he can feel useful again.

When her efficient routine is disrupted by Ray's constant need for attention, will Lorraine pander to his desires or make a clean break to get her life back?

Mistletoe Moments

Veronica and Owen are looking forward to a happy Christmas on The Close and, as their fortieth birthdays approach, some significant celebration will be required, but how can Veronica agree to her husband's life-changing request?

Their son, Travis, is due to take some important exams, but will he be able to concentrate when a serious crush derails his schedule?

The Christmas Miracle

When Diane decides to seek closure with a matter from her past, she unexpectedly finds herself on a journey she isn't prepared for.

Her granddaughter, Emma, has all the technical know-how to assist in the search, but is distracted by an intense - and highly unsuitable - romance.

All the books in

the Aegean Sun series

and the

Christmas on The Close series

are available on Kindle

through Amazon

Printed in Great Britain
by Amazon

67397894R00108